ES · LIVES · LIVES · LIVES ·

SAINT
THÉRÈSE
OF LISIEUX

General Editor: James Atlas

SAINT
THÉRÈSE
OF LISIEUX
KATHRYN
HARRISON

Weidenfeld & Nicolson
LONDON

First published in Great Britain in 2003 by
Weidenfeld & Nicolson

First published in USA in 2003 by Viking/Penguin

A CIP catalogue record for this book is available
from the British Library

ISBN 0 297 84728 7

Printed by Butler & Tanner Ltd, Frome and London

Weidenfeld & Nicolson

The Orion Publishing Group Ltd
Orion House
5 Upper Saint Martin's Lane
London
WC2H 9EA

For my father-in-law,
Earl Harrison,
a child of light

CONTENTS

How powerless I am to express in human
language the secrets of heaven.

—*Thérèse Martin*

Symptoms of disease are nothing but a
disguised manifestation of the power of love; and
all disease is only love transformed.

—*Thomas Mann*

SAINT THÉRÈSE OF LISIEUX

AT HER DEATH in 1897, it would seem that Thérèse Martin, twenty-four years old, had achieved all she'd set out to accomplish: nothingness, hiddenness, self denied to the point of invisibility. Many of the Carmelite nuns who had lived with her for nine years, sharing work and prayers and meals, reflected that they had hardly known her and, as one put it, 'would never have suspected her sanctity.'

Two years later, in 1899, the town of Lisieux was so inundated by pilgrims seeking Thérèse's relics that her grave had to be put under guard. The official beatification process was underway by 1910, the notoriously slow-moving Roman Curia scrambling to avoid being 'anticipated' by the 'voice of the people.' *Poor grain of sand, counted for nothing. Poor thread, under the feet of all. Poor atom, for whom contempt, insults, and humiliation were too glorious:* she was a celebrity with an international reputation for granting miracles.

On May 17, 1925, Sister Thérèse of the Child Jesus and of the Holy Face became Saint Thérèse of Lisieux, in the fastest canonization to date in the history of the Catholic Church. In

1997, to mark the centenary of her death, Pope John Paul II declared Thérèse a Doctor of the Church, a title bestowed on those few saints (only thirty-two thus far, of whom three are women) whose spiritual knowledge and teaching are deemed extraordinary.

The subject of countless biographies, Thérèse is herself a best-seller, her own words translated into nearly fifty languages, her effigy smiling down from altars all over the world, a miracle of deceptive sentimentality. Although she is popularly known as the Little Flower, a better name might be the Little Nettle: those who look beyond the smile to the doctrine will find themselves stung and provoked, and the discomfort takes its time to fade.

Much as she claimed to want to disappear among the unpublished, it was Saint Thérèse who did most of the work of turning herself into a readable and compelling text. *Springtime Story of a Little White Flower,* the title she gave to her autobiography, was written under obedience to her mother superior, who was also her elder sister Pauline. She wrote hurriedly during her one free hour each evening, an hour that came at the end of a long day of work and prayer and illness. A collection of 'thoughts on the graces God deigned to grant' her, the book was conceived for an intimate audience, Thérèse's four biological sisters. Only after she had completed it did she imagine that what she'd written might be useful to others – that among homely anecdotes, the seemingly casual references to grammar lessons and beach trips and even hair ribbons, she had carefully and minutely revealed her path towards 'nothingness.'

On September 30, 1898, exactly a year after her death, the 476-page account of her spiritual life was published. Edited, polished, and in some measure conventionalized and stripped of its spontaneity by Pauline, whom she named her literary executrix, it was sent to all the Carmel convents in France in lieu of a more standard obituary notice. The surplus of the run of two thousand copies sold for four francs apiece. Six months later, it was reprinted to satisfy demand; a subsequent edition included letters of praise from bishops and other members of the clergy. By 1915, nearly a million copies were in print; a separate publication anthologized the hundreds of thousands of letters (arriving at a rate of five hundred a day, one thousand a day by 1925) that bore witness to miracles granted by Thérèse's intercession.

Story of a Soul, as it was eventually titled, was not a novel, but it shared a romantic sensibility and cherished plot elements with immensely popular nineteenth-century fiction, books such as *Les Misérables, Little Women,* and *David Copperfield,* whose characters had entered the culture at large. Marrying romance to classic elements of hagiography – apparitions of the Virgin, temptations by the devil, symbolic dreams, presentiments of glory, conversion – Thérèse wrote of the death of her self-sacrificing and affectionate mother, of the devotion of her father, of her striving to become a saint, and of the reversals she suffered. Her life on the page was dramatized by the irresistible alchemy of tuberculosis, the same literary disease that ennobled and transfigured the heroines of Victor Hugo, Louisa May Alcott, and Charles Dickens, and that acted as a powerful accelerant in Thérèse's own corporeal and spiritual life. Unconsciously, Thérèse created a perfect vehicle for conveying the teachings of the Church, because she made the rigors of mysticism incidental to human drama.

Story of a Soul is a love story, a desperate and feverish one, involving tears and palpitations, wild hopes and bleak anguish, the audacity of a commoner who set her heart on a king, a child bride who, in her zeal for Christ, her beloved, defied one after another Church official until, at fourteen, she arrived in Rome to petition the pope to allow her premature entry into a convent. Consumers of more contemporary and conventional romance might find her narrative quaint and mannered, suffused with earnestness, lacking in irony. Reading Thérèse is akin to having a conversation with a disconcertingly precocious child; she has that quality of being awkward and artful at the same instant, forcing our abrupt awareness of both her depth and her vulnerability. She bares her soul, and to witness this is to realize how seldom humans do.

'To me it seemed like the story of a "steel bar",' Albino Luciani (who would later become Pope John Paul I) commented on the book's original title, succinctly identifying the paradox of the Little Flower. Few personalities have been so obscured by sentiment, few wills so cloaked by feminine convention. The romantic formulas that Thérèse used to tell her story contributed not only to its vast popularity, but also to the profound misunderstanding of an ambitious and intelligent young woman, a shy neurotic who fashioned a martyr's death from circumstances that threatened to withhold all means toward the glorious sainthood she envisioned for herself.

No one provides more stark an example of the radical nature of discipleship to Christ. 'If any man would come after me, let him deny himself,' Jesus admonished. 'Leave the dead to bury their own dead,' he told the would-be Christian, the one who wanted to first honor his biological father.

Is it possible to have a moderate belief in God? Can we believe in God and continue to live a life of moderation? 'They knew too well how to ally the joys of this earth to the service of God,' Thérèse said of the good Catholics in her hometown, separating herself from those who didn't look for total and obliterating union with the divine, who didn't believe that to love Christ demanded a complete sacrifice of self. Indeed, to her father's pious friends, the God of Thérèse Martin might have appeared as violent as the devil, her heaven as annihilating as the atheist's last breath.

LOOKING BACK on her life from the vantage of her twenty-two years, having arrived at a moment when, in her own estimation, she could 'cast a glance on the past,' she was able to divide it into distinct periods.

The first of these began and ended with her mother, Zélie.

Zélie, christened Marie-Azélie Guérin, was born in Orne, Normandy, in 1831, the middle child of a professional soldier, Isidore Guérin, and a woman of the peasant class, Louise-Jeanne Mace. At nineteen, Zélie applied as a postulant to the Sisters of Charity of Saint Vincent de Paul, envisioning a life of service to the sick and destitute. She believed she was called to this work; also, she sought a welcome and comfort in the Church that she had never received at home, refuge from a mother who indulged her one son and persecuted her daughters to the point that Zélie would one day recall a youth 'as sad as a shroud.' Sincere in her vocation, she was nonetheless refused. She was turned away so bluntly, and without explanation, that most accounts blame her cruel mother's secret meddling.

Without income or inheritance, Zélie didn't have the luxury of time to mourn. She applied herself to discovering the future. Would God reveal another, different path? 'See to the making of *Point d'Alençon*,' an inner voice answered. Obedient – inspired – Zélie enrolled in the famous lace-making school of Alençon, where she discovered a talent that allowed her, after only two years' study, to establish a business in her own home, accepting commissions and employing local workers to help execute her designs. Twenty-two years old, she began gathering the dowry her parents had denied her. She regarded her older sister's recent acceptance into the Visitation convent at Le Mans not with envy but with wistfulness. Her sister, Marie-Louise, intended, as she herself said, to become a saint. Zélie would have to content herself with a family, children she could consecrate to the will of God.

When Zélie's guiding voice sounded again, it used the language of annunciation, indicating Louis Martin as her husband-to-be. 'This is he whom I have prepared for you,' she heard as she passed the not-so-young gentleman on Alençon's Bridge of Saint Leonard. Was this an imagined introduction, an unconscious romantic embellishment? The location makes us wonder, for bridges are structures of union – connecting shores, leaping obstacles – archetypal meeting places for lovers, even lovers who are strangers.

The story of the courtship of Thérèse Martin's parents has come to us through their daughters, relayed in the same tone of inevitability as that which informs every creation myth, great and small. It is, perhaps, more true than factual. But wherever it occurred, a glance might have been enough to establish Zélie and Louis as kindred souls.

Louis Martin, born in 1823 in Bordeaux, was also the child of a soldier. His father, a captain in Napoleon's army, pursued a career that routinely uprooted his family. Still, ambitious for his son's future, on his retirement Captain Martin settled in Alençon for the educational resources it offered. Louis, artistic and melancholy, was not a gifted student, however. At twenty-two, he traveled from Normandy to the renowned Swiss monastery of Saint Bernard, attracted by the remote beauty of the Alps and the vision he had of himself helping travelers in need. Like his wife-to-be, Louis was rejected as a religious; unlike Zélie, he was given a reason: he did not know Latin.

Louis came home to study under a classics master and failed spectacularly, suffering a nervous collapse from the strain. Quiet and contemplative, when he recovered he settled on a trade that suited such a personality, a refined and meticulous trade similar to the one that occupied Zélie. After apprenticeships in Strasbourg and Paris, Louis returned to Alençon as a clock maker and jeweler, a man who fashioned his own retreat from the world, who marveled at the beauty of nature and refused the temptations of sex.

The match between Zélie Guérin and Louis Martin was facilitated by Louis's mother, then enrolled in the lace-making school, and on July 13, 1858, the two were married. The ceremony took place at midnight, as was the custom, in Alençon's Notre Dame cathedral, and the couple began their life together in material if not psychic comfort.

Having succumbed to a woman whose energy and determination would always direct their life together, for ten months Louis managed to hold Zélie to a 'Josephite,' or celibate, marriage (a term inspired by the traditional understanding of Joseph and Mary's abstention from intercourse). But after a grief-stricken visit to the Visitation convent to seek her sister's advice, Zélie took Louis to a confessor who affirmed that a committedly religious couple might undertake to populate the world with priests and nuns, even missionaries.

At last the saint's mother had embarked on what she would come to regard as a truer vocation than that of the cloister. Little more than a year after her marriage, Zélie was expecting a child, and her mother had died of congestion of the lungs. The desolation of her youth was over.

The Martins began by living with Louis's parents in their home on the rue du Pont Neuf. From 1866 until his death in 1868, they cared for Zélie's father in that house; in 1870, during the Franco-Prussian War, they were forced to provide lodging and meals for nine German soldiers. War brought dysentery, smallpox, looting. But for an overwhelmingly Catholic populace, the subsequent surge of Marxism and anticlerical rallies were nearly as destructive as war and epidemics, and they were hardly the first such aftershocks of the Revolution, now eighty years past.

What has been described as the 'dechristianization' of eighteenth-century France found a catalyst in the Revolution's interruption of church services and its suspension of religious education. Church and state were divorced; French citizens were no longer necessarily Catholic by virtue of being French. Massacres on both sides ensured that the predominantly royalist Catholics and the anticlerical (even agnostic or atheistic) republicans would regard each other with suspicion and hostility well into the twentieth century. As measured by falling attendance at Easter mass, fewer and fewer people were tolerant of a religion that denied earthly pleasures even as it looked forward to the punishments of purgatory or, worse, hell.

Seemingly untouched by the Enlightenment's call to reason, its optimism and humanism, the Martins were conservative, not only as measured against the citizens of Paris, fifty miles away, but even in their own provincial town of sixteen thousand. They understood themselves to be practicing a religion under siege and held more obdurately to the ancien régime obsession with corruption, its dualistic insistence that the soul is not housed but imprisoned by the body, its focus on death and damnation. Local custom allowed shops to stay open on Sunday – it was a day of leisure and spending during which a majority of Catholics did business – but Louis and Zélie remembered the Sabbath and kept it holy.

Alençon was, and remains, a picturesque medieval town, dominated by the cathedral where Louis and Zélie were married, where they went together at five every morning to attend mass. Each day began with the couple affirming, in the words of the Credo, 'the life of the world to come' and continued in a spirit of suspicion of the here and now. While the Martin family's livelihood depended on the creation of luxury items – lace, jewelry, fine clocks – and while they lived in solid bourgeois comfort, 'slaves to fashion,' as Zélie herself observed, they purposefully took limited pleasure in the material world. What they made and what they bought was tangible, and it was temporary. Against the eternity of God and of heaven, in which the Martins placed their hope, prosperity was of no consequence. As Teresa of Ávila, the great reformer of Carmel, famously remarked about the poverty of her cell, what difference was one short night spent in bad hostelry? Zélie Martin might have amended the saint's question to ask what could be gained by one night in a five-star hotel. Passing by a 'beautiful chateau and some magnificent properties,' Zélie told herself, 'All this is nothing. We shall not be happy until all of us . . . are reunited up above.'

On earth, Zélie worked to the point of exhaustion, often until midnight, piecing together lace for her commissions. While the pious might frown on social ambition, they understood poverty as a punishment for sin; and for the Martins a sizable income was necessary. In the space of thirteen years Louis and Zélie had nine children: Marie in 1860; Pauline, 1861; Léonie, 1863; Hélène, 1864; Joseph Louis, 1866; Joseph Jean-Baptiste, 1867; Céline, 1869; Mélanie, 1870; and Thérèse in 1873. Of the nine, five girls – Marie, Pauline, Léonie, Céline, and Thérèse – survived infancy, although each in her turn frightened her mother by succumbing to the expected childhood ailments.

Despite her worries and her periods of mourning, one running into another, despite the exhaustion of nine pregnancies and nine confinements, of days and nights sacrificed to the care of the moribund, Zélie was unreserved in her devotion to her family. 'I am madly in love with children,' she wrote her sister-in-law, 'I was born to have them.' But while she invested her prayers and hopes in her sickly babies, it was her atelier that prospered, to the point that Louis had to keep her books as well as travel to Paris to buy materials and meet with salespeople. Eventually, with his jeweler's eye, Louis took a hand in the design and manufacture of the lace, and by 1870 he had sold his business to direct his wife's. By virtue of talent and determination, Zélie had created the kind of family business the French typically hold in high esteem, and yet she never spoke of it with pride but called it the 'crown upon all my misfortunes.'

In a letter to her brother in 1865, Zélie had made a deliberately measured reference to a 'glandular swelling' in one of her breasts, an inflammation she traced to a girlhood injury. The site caused her pain and intermittent numbness, but she lacked confidence in the local physicians. She wasn't afraid of surgery; still, what time did she have to seek treatment in Paris?

The swelling was cancer, and the tumor, though it grew slowly, hindered Zélie from nursing all but the first of her children, leaving the young family dependent on wet nurses. Hired by many bourgeois to convey status and prosperity, a wet nurse was a necessity rather than a luxury for the Martins. Rose Taillé, who lived in the neighboring town of Semallé, took Zélie's two boys into her home and cared for them scrupulously. But their deaths – Joseph Louis's in 1867 from a streptococcal infection, Joseph Jean-Baptiste's in 1868 from bronchitis – devastated Zélie, who made one after another panicked early morning and late evening trip between Alençon and Semallé. It was nearly five miles, and she often went by herself, on foot, in the dark, in ice or rain; the weather didn't concern her. 'I was not frightened and would have crossed a forest alone,' she said. But when Mélanie was born in 1870, amid the unrest of the German occupation, she determined to keep the baby at home and looked for a nurse who was willing to live under the same roof. Unfortunately, there was no such woman, and the closest she could find, on Alençon's rue de la Barre, was not close enough. Unsupervised, the nurse neglected the infant, and Mélanie, whose parents sat down to dine on mahogany chairs, died of starvation, a mere seven and a half months after the sudden death of her five-year-old sister Hélène following less than a day of unexplained illness.

'People said to me,' Zélie wrote her sister-in-law, "It would have been better never to have had them.' I couldn't stand such language. . . . They were not lost forever.' Zélie prayed to her babies, her holy innocents. She looked forward to her reunion with them in heaven.

And yet she admitted she was 'terrified of death . . . arms so stiff and face so cold!' Pregnant again in 1872, Zélie girded herself with her older sister's prophetic insistence that she would one day give birth to a great saint. The family had recently moved into a house at 36, rue Saint Blaise, which Zélie inherited from her father; perhaps life would assume the comfortable aspect of the new dwelling. Zélie did not allow herself or Louis to succumb to worries over her own compromised health or to the equally reasonable fears about the vulnerable creature she carried within her. Instead, she understood her last pregnancy, with Thérèse, to be charged with supernatural significance. One evening, immersed in a spiritual text, she found herself wondering about the demonic attacks suffered by saints and reassured herself that, being of limited spiritual stature, she would never be persecuted in this way. No sooner had she relaxed than she felt a great clawing weight on her shoulder, like that of a talon, pain she would later interpret as a warning from the devil, a sign of his displeasure with the holy child she would bring to life. Thérèse, not yet born, was already a prodigy; and Zélie reported with astonishment 'something which never happened with my other children, when I sang, she sang with me.'

The voice of holiness announced itself. If this is maternal fancy – and a contemporary audience does insist on psychology before marvels – still it betrays something important: even before Thérèse was born, Zélie was besotted with her last child. She felt a transcendent bond with the little girl whom she would come to describe as remarkable in every way. Smarter, prettier, sweeter, more willful than her other children, and already consecrated to God.

AT HER BIRTH, on January 2, 1873, Thérèse weighed eight pounds. 'Everyone tells me she is beautiful,' Zélie exulted. The infant was baptized on January 4 in the cathedral where her parents were married. Her sister Marie, nearly thirteen, was made her godmother. Greeted with enormous affection and pride by parents old enough to be grandparents (Louis was nearly fifty, Zélie forty-one), at twelve days old Thérèse already smiled at her mother with recognition. 'I thought I was mistaken,' Zélie wrote her brother and sister-in-law of the baby's impossible precociousness, 'but I could no longer doubt it yesterday.'

A week later, Thérèse was gravely ill. Unwilling to open her home to the danger of 'an unsuitable person as all wet-nurses today are,' Zélie wrote to her sister-in-law that she had been feeding Thérèse 'toast with water, with half milk; this is her entire nourishment.' Intestinal inflammation, increasing weakness: Thérèse was failing so quickly that her mother, fearing her imminent death, made the wrenching decision to separate herself from her infant daughter. On March 15, 1873, she sent her to Rose Taillé, who, with a baby of her own, was unable to live in town with the Martins. Barely two and a half months old, Thérèse suffered the first of a series of dramatic separations, exiles that would form her personality, her understanding of mortality and of salvation, of hope and of heaven and hell.

In the country, Thérèse recovered and thrived. Even so, the year she spent in the Taillés' small brick farmhouse was a hard and humiliating one for Zélie. On Thursdays, Rose Taillé brought the child to market in Alençon, and, not surprisingly, Zélie found that the baby – 'very gay, very darling' – clung to Rose while rejecting her mother. She wouldn't allow Zélie to take her home for an afternoon and cried piteously when she could no longer see the wet nurse. Afraid of a mother wearing the stylish fashions of the town, Thérèse preferred to be held by women dressed like Rose, in country clothes.

As with every passage of her life, the year Thérèse spent in Semallé is well documented. Zélie Martin had a gift for observation and narrative and wrote frequently to her two eldest daughters, Marie and Pauline, boarders at the Visitation convent school in Le Mans, and to her brother's wife in Lisieux, Céline Guérin, a woman with whom she obviously felt kinship. The 217 letters that have been preserved are filled with anecdotes about Thérèse and her sisters, as well as wry glances at the local gentry. Having suffered much, Zélie understood there was no guarantee of happiness on earth, and even her gossip betrays a sometimes smug suspicion of mortal pleasures. When Monsieur and Madame C. exulted over a fine house they were building and one dark night fell together into a ditch on the construction site, subsequently dying of the injuries they sustained, Zélie ended her report to her brother with a tart 'there you have the lamentable story of this so-happy couple.' She could not tell an amusing story without extracting a moral, and the moral was often that only fools looked for comfort in the present.

Without Zélie, without the consciousness that could evoke misery with the swift economy of a phrase like 'sad as a shroud,' there would be no narrative tradition in the Martin family. After Zélie died, her expressive and compelling voice remained among the husband and daughters who mourned her. Her letters were treasured and read aloud to the younger girls, who listened and learned to speak their mother's language, to understand the world and the will of God as their mother herself had understood it. Echoed by all of her daughters, written into their correspondence, quoted everywhere in *Story of a Soul,* Zélie's words guided the vocations of all five of the children who survived her. More forcefully than the grip of an angry demon, or the prophecy of a dying nun, they articulated the arrival of a saint.

At the end of April 1874, Thérèse came home to Alençon. Fifteen months old, in sound physical health, still she had suffered a second disorienting loss, both of the breast and of the woman who she necessarily believed was her mother. Zélie wrote to her older daughters that their sister 'does not want to leave me, she is continually with me; she loves going into the garden very much, but if I am not there, she does not want to remain and cries until someone brings her back to me.'

17

All children must negotiate separation, of course, but the little girl Zélie described was particularly vigilant and wary. Standing on the stairs, nearly two years old, Thérèse would not go up or down without 'calling at each step Mamma, Mamma! So many steps, so many Mamma's!' If Zélie failed to answer, Thérèse did not move. In a rare moment of obtuseness – or perhaps denial, both of her pain and of her child's – Zélie complained of Thérèse's clinging, as if she did not understand its source.

Already, before the age of three, Thérèse was speaking in complex and surprising sentences. 'In her transports of love,' Zélie reported, Thérèse wished her mother and father dead – 'since you say we must die to go there,' the little girl explained, referring, as she often did, to heaven. Increasingly, much of Thérèse's conversation – all that her mother found worth transcribing – concerned religion. Heaven, hell, reward, punishment: she was high-spirited, 'full of life' as she later described herself, but she was not carefree. She pushed her sister; she slapped her sister; she tore the wallpaper; she broke a vase. When she misbehaved, she was immediately overcome by a remorse disconcerting in a person so young. 'She is a child who becomes easily overexcited,' Zélie wrote Pauline in May of 1876. 'As soon as she has done something wrong everybody must know it. . . . she has in her little mind that we will pardon her more easily if she accuses herself.'

Reading such accounts, stories later retold and amplified by her sisters, one is tempted to conclude that Thérèse's first sins were inspired by her need to confess and thus to rehearse a dynamic that would always possess her: a cycle of transgression, alienation, confession, and finally – blessedly – reunion. She always betrayed a great deal more pleasure in confession, in the reinstatement and safety granted by confession, than in whatever sin occasioned the need to confess. A stolen sweet, a lie, an act of calculated disobedience: these typical little misdeeds, against which an ordinary child might weigh the prospect of punishment, were not Thérèse's brand of naughtiness. She was impulsive; she had a violent temper. When frustrated, she 'rolls on the floor like one in despair, believing that all is lost,' her mother recounted. Sometimes, she even choked.

Each having been denied life as a religious, at home Louis and Zélie Martin created an atmosphere of faith and piety that few convents could rival. But they were not dour, nor ascetic in their faith. Sunday was greeted as a holiday, with hot chocolate in bed, curled hair and pretty dresses, the intoxication of music and incense at mass, followed by an extravagant meal and the pleasure of a long walk in one another's company. Every feast day was welcomed as an opportunity to renew one's ardor and commitment to God, and Zélie outspokenly preferred that her daughters die young and virtuous than that they thrive outside the faith. The four children who did die were petitioned in heaven as saints, receiving the supplication of family they left behind. In such a context, it isn't surprising that Thérèse, already once abandoned and reclaimed, would learn to translate every act and its consequence into the arena of sin and redemption, but Zélie's reports of what she saw as a precocious religious sensibility might equally reveal a fearful, even desperate personality.

Closest to Céline, who was only three years older, Thérèse attached herself to her sister with characteristic resolve. She sat, not moving, for two or more hours in the schoolroom at home, sometimes weeping with fatigue and frustration but determined not to be denied the privilege of listening as Céline did her lessons with Marie, home from boarding school. Rather than stay at the dinner table alone, she left her dessert to be with Céline, and the two little girls amused themselves in the small back garden where Louis had put up a swing. Thérèse was shy, afraid to cross the street to play with the prefect's daughter in her big house and park, but she had physical courage. Tied into the swing with a rope, she screamed when it didn't go high enough to suit her. Céline was older, but she made an impression altogether fainter than did Thérèse, who was obstinate, imaginative, passionate, and determined to get her way.

The two youngest looked forward to the elder girls' holidays from convent school, from which Marie brought home a little string of beads, a chaplet on which she taught Céline to count up her 'acts of virtue.' Each time Céline conquered self-love, each time she sacrificed her desires to those of another, she could slip her hand in her pocket and move one bead forward. As it was impossible to leave Thérèse out of so irresistible and significant a game – the tallying up of worthiness – she also was given a set of beads and soon outstripped Céline in the practice of virtue. 'She records even a little too much,' Zélie thought, a noteworthy judgment from such a mother. 'Her chaplet of practices never leaves her for one minute.' Perhaps more portentous, as Marie would reflect after Thérèse's death, her pride was such that, even at three, the sacrifice of her own will required that she do violence to herself.

To test the mettle of her daughter, Zélie offered Thérèse a sou to kiss the floor. Thérèse refused. 'When she says no, nothing can make her give in,' Zélie wrote Pauline. 'I could put her all day in the cellar and she would rather sleep there than say "yes".' Offered to choose what she wanted from among a basket of ribbons and doll clothes, Thérèse didn't follow the example of Céline's polite restraint; she didn't select one or even two but grabbed the whole thing. Her temperament was not formed for compromise or moderation, and writing the story of her soul, she chose this incident as 'a summary of my whole life,' a life spent not taming but directing her appetite and her will, a life perhaps shortened by the force of her desire and ambition.

Zélie continued to assess her daughter's moral progress, and she was equally vigilant about her frail health. Thérèse had one respiratory complaint after another, some so severe they caused her difficulty in breathing that lasted for months and a 'strange whistling in her chest' when she walked quickly. No remedy could repair such a constitution, and each cold, each fever frightened Zélie, whose thoughts turned quickly to death, perhaps influencing the games of Céline and Thérèse. Pretend funerals were a favorite. 'Truly the burial of a doll is very amusing,' her sister Marie wrote a friend. 'Thérèse has experienced this more than once.'

Mothers and daughters wrote one another leisurely detailed accounts of ordinary days, but as few long, personal letters from Louis Martin exist, our vision of Thérèse's father is one reflected by the women who surrounded him. By all accounts, he was completely in love with his youngest daughter. He was her 'King of France and Navarre' – a name she would always use for him – and she was his Little Queen or, in another mood, his Benjamin (the youngest son of Jacob, whose 'portion was five times as much'). When Zélie worried about a threat to her daughter's life, she could not consider her own grief before she thought of how bereft would be Thérèse's father, who 'adores her! . . . It is incredible all the sacrifices he makes for her day and night.'

Dignified, white-haired Louis Martin rode Thérèse through town on his shoulders and took her for walks and to his special sanctuary, the Pavilion on the rue des Lavoirs. A whimsical six-sided tower surrounded by fields and a stream, the Pavilion was where Louis kept his angling gear, where he relaxed and mused, and where Thérèse enjoyed picking strawberries. A gifted mimic, Louis filled the house with games and play alien to Zélie's more sober nature. And he put his faith into practice: he encouraged the giving of alms, provided food and shelter to those in need, helped carry the sacraments to the ill, the dying. He welcomed as a holy privilege his part in the spiritual guidance of so beautiful and prepossessing a daughter.

What was to become of Thérèse? Zélie wondered in a letter to Pauline. 'I do not know too well how she will turn out,' she wrote, trying to predict the impact of 'superior intelligence' on 'invincible stubbornness.' At three and a half, the child was beginning to read, and she understood ideas as complex and as abstract as omnipotence, which she explained to Céline, who couldn't see how God could be present in the communion wafers, when He was so big and the host so small. 'This is not surprising since God is all-powerful,' Thérèse said.

'What does all-powerful mean?' Céline asked.

'It means to do whatever He wills!'

'Thérèse asked me the other day if she would go to heaven,' Zélie wrote to Pauline on October 29, 1876, less than a year before her own death. 'I told her yes, if she were very good. She answered, 'Yes, but if I were not good, I would go to hell . . . but I know what I would do. I would fly to you who would be in heaven. What would God do to take me? You would hold me tightly in your arms.' I saw in her eyes that she positively believed that God could do nothing to her if she were in the arms of her mother.'

IN JUNE of 1877, Zélie Martin, accompanied by her three older daughters, made a pilgrimage to Lourdes. For a woman of apparently unfaltering faith, it was not a desperate act but acknowledgment that her illness was no longer one that so comparatively weak a recourse as medicine could address. The Church was dismissive of science and technological advance; any medicine unaided by God would fail, while God unaided by medicine remained omnipotent. After eleven years of relative dormancy, the tumor had metastasized; Zélie's entire breast was enlarged and tender; the flesh on her neck and back was discolored; she suffered numbness on one side, an unremitting ache, periods of incapacitating pain. She consulted a physician in Alençon and another in Lisieux, where her brother and sister-in-law lived. Both doctors judged that the time for surgery had long passed; there was nothing they could do to help her. Zélie prayed for more time with her family – she felt her middle child, Léonie, needed her especially – but she was accepting of whatever was God's will.

'It seems impossible that I can go away,' she wrote her

sister-in-law from Lourdes, wondering how her family would manage without her. 'Then I think that I must remain and shall remain. I am like all those I have known, not realizing their own state. Only others can see clearly, and one is amazed how the patients promise themselves an indefinite time whereas their days are numbered. It is curious indeed, but I am like all the rest.'

The trip was made for an unhappy reason, and it was marked by inconvenience and discomfort. The train jolted and pitched on the rails, increasing Zélie's agonies and making her daughters ill; there was confusion over the lodgings; the food was bad; two cherished rosaries were lost; Zélie fell and twisted her neck badly; the waters themselves were punishingly cold. Still, Zélie managed to go into the grotto's pool four times. Once, she immersed herself for a quarter of an hour, too cold to feel anything while in the water, but when she got out 'the sharp twinges returned as usual.'

Zélie wasn't counting on a miraculous cure for herself; but as long as she was at Lourdes with Léonie, she poured water over the fourteen-year-old's head and begged the mercies of the Virgin to help her troubled child. Sandwiched between the older and wiser pair, on whom Zélie already counted as surrogates and teachers, and the petted babies, admired and much praised for their precocious virtue, Léonie had always been the odd child out among the five Martin daughters. Described as intellectually inferior, at least in comparison with her four sisters, she'd suffered a succession of ailments that had disrupted her early schooling and perhaps degraded her temperament. In the words of her exasperated mother, she was 'a model of insubordination,' antisocial and excitable, a moody, sullen shadow thrown into relief by the obedient, bright beams of those around her.

'You know what your sister was like,' Zélie wrote Pauline a few months before the trip to Lourdes. 'She would do the precise contrary of what I wished, even when she would have wished to do the thing asked of her. In short, she obeyed only the maid.'

During the last years of her mother's illness, Léonie had in fact been turned over to the maid, Louise Marais, who took pride in her ability to control a girl everyone else had failed to discipline. But Louise's success was that of the secret sadist, who terrorized Léonie with threats of violent punishments. With Zélie overwhelmed by other responsibilities – an attempt to sell the lace business fell through – Léonie and Louise seem to have found a perverse satisfaction in their liaison, not a happy one, to be sure, but a symbiosis that eclipsed the powerful Zélie, further exalted by her martyrdom. The sly and brutal game continued until Marie, having overheard what struck her as a disturbing exchange between the two, eaves-dropped until she learned more.

Louise was fired, the prodigal daughter gathered in, kissed and petted and prayed over, anointed with Lourdes water. The treatment worked – at least it effected a reunion between mother and daughter – but it also backfired. Léonie, appar-ently broken, having failed to thwart Zélie, now despaired at the imminent and unmanageably huge loss of her mother. 'Everyone cried,' Zélie wrote her sister-in-law of the scene in which she shared her doctors' pessimism with her family, 'Léonie sobbed.'

'I am very necessary to this child,' she confided to Pauline.

'After I am gone she will be too unhappy and no one will be able to make her obey.'

Léonie would suffer tribulations, certainly. But they would not be so simple as a failure of obedience. While her four sisters, first the elder pair and then the younger, entered the Lisieux Carmel, Léonie made one attempt after another at the religious life. In 1886, she briefly entered the Poor Clares at Alençon. In 1887, in 1893, and finally, successfully, in 1895, she was a postulant at the Visitation at Caen. She seems never to have had her sisters' (and perhaps many nuns') ability to project the idea of mother onto the ready canvas of the Church. Was this because she lacked the cohesive, uncomplicated vision of maternal love and power that the other four Martin girls shared?

Zélie returned to a summer of dire suffering, physical torment she accepted with a stoicism that Thérèse, perhaps too young to remember consciously, would nevertheless recapitulate in her own agonies, twenty years later.

Spiritually, Zélie was resigned to death. She believed in God and in resurrection, she had long placed her hope in the joys of heaven; she was able to understand physical torture as useful, productive: a means toward sanctification, a shortcut through purgatory. But the burdens of each day reminded her how dependent a family she had created. Louis was unable to conceal his grief and was 'inconsolable . . . as though completely crushed.' It was obvious to Zélie's brother, Isidore, and to his wife, Céline, that the father would be unable to hold the family together, and they encouraged a move to Lisieux after Zélie's death. There the girls would find a 'second mother in their aunt.'

Zélie's final weeks were marked by a suffering that left an indelible trauma. In too much pain to lie down, too much pain to sleep, she 'went from bed to the armchair and from the armchair to bed.' In order to spare her the added irritant of noise, people whispered around the dying woman and took off their shoes. Over and over, Zélie repeated the words of Saint Francis de Sales: 'One ounce of virtue practiced in tribulation is worth more than a thousand in times of peace and joy.' Marie and Pauline remained at home to attend to their mother. Léonie came up with the only solution that would end her own and her family's grief – she offered God her life in exchange for her mother's, sincerely enough that she immediately felt ill and believed in her approaching death. Each morning Céline and Thérèse were sent off with Madame Leriche, a cousin by marriage who impressed the children primarily in the many ways she was different from their mother. Aware that a crisis was occurring and that they were shuffled aside, Thérèse later called herself and her sister 'two poor little *exiles*,' a word and an idea that recur throughout her writings. Exile from mother was immediately translated into exile from safety, succor, comfort, God. As it would be for any four-year-old.

But Thérèse Martin's conception of heaven would remain unashamedly anthropomorphic and personal: the restoration of family – mother, father, and all nine children reunited before God, God as indistinguishable from father as the Virgin from mother. Before this reunion was to happen, however, Thérèse would endure and then learn to embrace twenty years of suffering.

Up to the point of her mother's death, Thérèse described her early years in the words of Zélie, stories corroborated and enhanced by her sisters. When she faulted her three-year-old self for vanity, the judgment came from an often-told account of her taking exaggerated pleasure in a pretty blue dress. As it is for most of us, her autobiography was informed – formed – by family reminiscences, handled and rehandled, scenes tumbling like stones through a stream of collective narrative. Received by us, they have a smooth and even slippery quality, no purchase left, no snag of immediacy or individual authenticity. But Zélie's death changed that, just as it changed everything: it provided the saint her first autonomous memory, even as it was an event that almost defied articulation. It was so large, and Thérèse's talent was in evoking the minute.

'I don't recall having cried very much, neither did I speak to anyone about the feelings I experienced. I looked and listened in silence,' she would later write.

By August 26, having suffered a hemorrhage, Zélie was confined to bed, her limbs too weak and too swollen to support her. Thérèse watched as her mother was given the last rites, all five of the Martin daughters lined up by age: Marie, seventeen; Pauline, sixteen; Léonie, fourteen; Céline, seven; and, last of all, Thérèse, four and a half. Standing at the elbow of the priest, Louis sobbed aloud. Zélie died the next day, just after midnight. On the morning of August 28, carried in her father's arms, Thérèse kissed her mother's corpse. With the family preoccupied by the crisis at hand, she had the opportunity to measure herself against the waiting coffin lid. 'I had to raise my head to take in its full height. It appeared large and dismal.'

The funeral took place on August 29 at Our Lady's Cemetery in Alençon. Afterward, as family lore presented the scene, Louise Marais, the maid who had been fired for persecuting Léonie, looked at Céline and Thérèse and remarked, 'Poor little ones, you no longer have a mother!' at which point Céline threw herself into Marie's arms and said, 'Well you shall be my mama!' and Thérèse ran to the second sister saying, 'For me, Pauline will be Mama!' It's interesting that Louise was made a catalyst for the one dying wish Zélie had reiterated. Did this redeem the amoral maid, did it defeat her more thoroughly, did it accomplish both ends? In any case, the elder girls had already promised their mother to guide and catechize their little sisters, but not even as devoted a surrogate as Pauline could assuage so devastating a loss.

By her own account, proved in every detail of her subsequent life, the death of Zélie had a radical and destructive effect on Thérèse. 'My happy disposition' (a happiness the observant reader has cause to question, a disposition already complicated by fear and even rage) was 'completely changed,' Thérèse recalled. Having been joyful and extroverted, she became 'timid and retiring, sensitive to an excessive degree.' It would require what she regarded as a miracle to restore her original nature.

IMMEDIATELY AFTER the death of his wife, Louis moved his family to Lisieux, where Zélie's brother and sister-in-law lived. The successful sale of Zélie's lace-making business and of the family's three properties in Alençon gave him ample resources to lease a large home on the outskirts of town and to hire a maid to help with the care of his children. He relied on the proximity of the Guérins, especially Céline, with whom Zélie had shared so many of her concerns and joys as a mother, to help fill the void left by his wife's absence. Léonie went to board at the local Benedictine abbey school. Marie and Pauline undertook the education, respectively, of Céline and Thérèse.

Without the social intercourse demanded by a business in the luxury trade – supplying lace for gowns and trousseaux – the Martin home was more than ever a place of preparation for the cloister all five girls would ultimately choose. To reach the new house, called Les Buissonnets, or 'the little shrubbery,' one took 'a stony path that ran steeply uphill.' In contrast to the Alençon house on the busy rue Saint Blaise, Les

Buissonnets was enclosed by a high wall and included a big private garden, suiting Louis Martin's determination to shield his five daughters from 'anything which he thought might be an occasion of temptation,' as Marie said. His protectiveness would be guided by the wisdom of the Church, whose clergy warned of conspiracies to corrupt the faithful by means of *les mauvaises lectures,* novels that might seduce young women and lead them astray, much as they had Emma Bovary, books that Louis made sure never penetrated Les Buissonnets. All the sisters would remember their father's absolute devotion, his sensitivity to his children's needs, his self-sacrificing nature. 'Our father's very affectionate heart seemed to be enriched now with a truly maternal love,' Thérèse wrote. And yet the second period of her life, the one she was to identify as the most painful, had begun.

Each morning, Thérèse was woken and dressed by Pauline, with whom she said her prayers. After breakfast she had lessons with her chosen mother – 'the first word I was able to read without help was 'heaven'' – crying over her grammar, enjoying history and catechism. Life in the Martin family offered the solace of routine and seemed to accommodate with grace the indulging of the youngest. Perhaps because the family ethos didn't permit jealousy, perhaps because Thérèse was so obviously vulnerable in her grief, her four older sisters didn't begrudge her an extra measure of affection but followed their father's example, petting and praising, echoing Zélie's judgment that Thérèse was superior in virtue and intelligence.

Such gifts, however, granted no leniency. Pauline undertook the education of her little sister with all the conscientious self-importance of a sixteen-year-old. For the next four years, until she was twenty and Thérèse was eight, she explained and quizzed and catechized, pouring what she'd learned in boarding school into the eager vessel of a child who lived to please, a child who could arrive at safety only through virtue and accomplishment. When, in 1910, Pauline gave testimony at the beatification process, she remembered Thérèse's unfailing obedience – 'she asked permission for everything' – and spoke of training her in humility and sacrifice.

Thérèse wanted to know how it was that God chose among souls, heaping more favors upon some than others, and Pauline answered the question with a mug and a thimble. Filling each to the brim, she asked her pupil which was the fuller. Neither. Both. It was a seminal image, one of the formative 'littlenesses' which would give rise to a doctrine. Souls might differ in magnitude, but each had the capacity to be totally filled by grace, 'the last having nothing to envy in the first.'

Thérèse earned her good grades in the form of wooden tokens, which she might redeem for an afternoon walk with her father. The two of them stopped at parks and at one or more of the town's churches; on the way home, Louis bought her a little gift, a pastry perhaps, an indulgent trifle. Remembered by Pauline as intensely 'sensitive to other people's sufferings,' Thérèse particularly enjoyed giving money to beggars and cripples. Vain in her own estimation, she looked forward to being seen in the company of her father. She was proud of the image they presented, his dignified bearing and snowy hair, her ribbons and curls and pretty dresses, their two hands joined in affection. And she must have been conscious of the favor of Louis's singular attention; after all, Thérèse had been chosen among five daughters. But what she would later confess as vanity strikes a questioning reader as a quite different brand of self-consciousness. Was it admiration she wanted, or was it witness? Better, *witnesses* – as if the more people who noticed father and daughter on their cherished walks, the more real the experience became for Thérèse, the more assured and habitual, the more permanent. What could tear her from the safety of her father's company? After they returned home, Thérèse played in the walled garden, where she devised little altars.

Allowed as a special treat to accompany Louis on a fishing trip, Thérèse didn't fish or even play in the water but sank into a melancholy state she would identify later as prayer, meditations on mortality in which even a stale jam sandwich gave her cause to grieve. 'Instead of the lively colors it had earlier, I saw now only a rosy tint and the bread had become old and crumbled. Earth again seemed a sad place.'

Following Zélie's powerful example, amplified by Pauline's seemingly humorless transmission of all the older girl had learned from their pious mother, Thérèse wrung moral significance from every event. In her *Story of a Soul*, she described a 'fault' that merited confession, that gave her the opportunity to reflect on the quality of her contrition.

As she often did when the older members of the family went to church, Thérèse, six years old, occupied herself with her own miniature altar, on which she had placed flowerpots and a candlestick, everything, as she said, 'arranged according to my taste.' Her precise and detailed description, fifteen years later, of these objects and of her pleasure in their size and perfection (in her notebooks she underscored the words *precious* and *little*) betrays fetishism. A psychic pressure behind the words suggests the altar had a power beyond the prosaic, accepted one. Sometimes, rarely, as Thérèse remembered, the maid Victoire would give her candle stubs. But on this occasion, the May devotions – May being the month dedicated to the Virgin, to Mother – Thérèse didn't expect any such favors, and she lit her 'precious tapers' (analogous to matches) and asked Victoire to begin the Memorare with her.

Remember, O most gracious Virgin Mary, that never was it known that anyone who fled to thy protection, implored thy help, or sought thy intercession was left unaided. Inspired with this confidence, I fly to thee, O Virgin of virgins, my Mother; to thee do I come; before thee I stand, sinful and sorrowful. O Mother of the Word Incarnate, despise not my petitions, but in thy mercy hear and answer me.

The maid, who had a tendency to tease, didn't say the words but remained silent; the matches rapidly burned away; and Thérèse succumbed to disproportionate rage. Rising from her knees, she 'shouted at [Victoire] and told her she was very wicked ... [she] stamped [her] foot with all [her] might.'

Shocked, Victoire held out two candle stubs, and Thérèse 'poured out tears of repentance.'

The adult Thérèse recounted the incident as an example of her temper and of her subsequent readiness to humble herself, but how unforgiving and dangerous a world the six-year-old must have faced to make her so desperate to have her prayers – supplications to a Mother in heaven she was

35

encouraged to confuse and conflate with her own – proceed without a hitch.

At the end of each day Thérèse asked Pauline, 'Was I very good?' and if the answer was not yes, she spent the night in tears. Frightened of the dark, she was eventually cured, or at least acclimated to shadows, by Pauline's program of behavior modification that sent Thérèse on brief evening errands into unlit rooms of the house.

Sunday remained her favorite day, the celebration of dressing for church, of becoming the Little Queen her father called her. Almost as rewarding as Sunday was illness, when Pauline 'gave her everything she wanted,' when she didn't have to be alone at night, but slept in her sister's bed – an 'incomparable favor.' Consistently, the experiences Thérèse treasured were those that offered the closest communion with the family she loved.

Evenings brought checkers and sitting on her father's lap with Céline. 'I cannot say how much I loved Papa,' Thérèse recalled. 'Everything in him caused me to admire him.' Louis Martin recited poetry, Lamartine and Victor Hugo, and he sang 'in his beautiful voice' the 'Song of the Angels' and other 'airs that filled the soul with profound thoughts.'

There are few supernatural events associated with Saint Thérèse – few before her death – but her biographers have minutely examined those she reported, leaning heavily upon them to render significance. The first was a prophetic vision Thérèse experienced during the summer of 1879 or 1880. She was six (or seven), and her father was in Alençon on business.

Thérèse, 'alone at the window of an attic,' saw a man dressed exactly like her father in front of the laundry shed in the far corner of the back garden. 'The man had the same height and walk as Papa, only he was much more stooped. His head was covered with a sort of apron.' Terrified, Thérèse called out to the apparition, loudly enough that she startled her sister Marie, who was downstairs and who noted the fear in her voice. But the bent man kept walking as if he hadn't heard her cries, and Thérèse watched as he passed behind some trees. She waited to see the figure reemerge, but he did not.

With her sister and the maid, Thérèse went to the garden to look for any sign of the apparition, but there was none. Over quickly, the vision remained 'engraved so deeply' on her heart. Years later, after her father suffered a series of paralytic strokes and periods of madness during which he tried to cloak his humiliation by hanging a handkerchief over his face, Thérèse interpreted what she saw as a warning God had given her of her father's tribulation and death.

A prophecy understood only after its subject has come to pass might be more projection than prediction. But Thérèse's fear of losing her King, the man on whom she based her idea of God, was real. When her father asked her to move from beneath a ladder on which he was standing, she stepped closer. 'If I fall, I'll crush you,' he warned, but she 'experienced an interior revulsion' and held tight to the ladder, thinking, 'I'll not have the grief of seeing him die; I'll die with him!'

At seven, Thérèse made her first confession; she was so small that to be heard she could not kneel within the booth but had to speak through the shutter standing up. Carefully prepared by Pauline's instruction, she understood that the ear of the priest on the other side of the partition was that of God, and she 'wondered whether she ought to tell him that she loved him with all her heart.' What she wanted was to receive communion, which Pauline had described as the beginning of 'a new life.' With four years to wait, she appropriated the experience of Céline's communion, vicariously 'inundated with joy. . . . It seemed as if it was I.' She remembered Céline's day as 'one of the most beautiful of my life.' More than eager, Thérèse was voracious and would participate fully in every religious step Céline took, eventually outdistancing and guiding her older sibling; but her identification was not complete, nor was it indiscriminate. Of all the Martins, it was Céline who would be tempted by romance and secular pleasures, which Thérèse would reject as violently as she embraced piety.

Even a trip to her uncle Isidore's house seemed filled with worldly corruption. Her mother's brother held her in his lap and frightened her with a song about Bluebeard, that rapacious and exciting sexual predator. Her cousins Jeanne and Marie Guérin danced quadrilles and involved themselves in childish intrigues from which Thérèse held herself aloof, suffering both her pride and her isolation.

If she was an unusual child, her early education and her separation from other children made her more peculiar still, both in what concerned her and in how she expressed herself. By her own admission, she did not know how to play and considered games a form of penance; and when in her turn she entered the Benedictine abbey school, she was miserable. She wasn't a boarder, as Léonie had been, but she found the eight hours of the school day an almost unbearably long punishment, especially because it began over again each morning.

Pauline had taught Thérèse too well, and she was put in a class with girls as much as five years older than she. Priggish, humorless, she was the butt of teasing. And she was without ability to defend herself against the fickle – 'narrow and flighty' – hearts of little girls. She befriended one who lost interest in her, and that was the last friend of her life. Henceforth, Jesus allowed her to find 'only bitterness in earth's friendships.' Uncharacteristically, her writing on the topic is neither generous nor sympathetic and betrays her vulnerability as a person of no social ease, with zero capacity to cope with rejection and separation – commonplaces of human relationships. Other children ran and skipped rope in the yard; Thérèse occupied herself with funerals for dead birds.

THÉRÈSE LOOKED BACK on the five years she spent at school as the 'saddest in my life,' years that taught her nothing more profoundly than they did her own alienation from the world. The teachers found her as odd as did the pupils – 'meticulously faithful to the smallest detail of the rules,' one recalled after her death, 'quiet, calm and reserved . . . dreamy.' Walking home one night from the Guérins' with her father, she saw a constellation of stars forming the letter *T:* proof that a great and shining apotheosis awaited her. On earth she was more than ever bereft when, in the summer of 1882, Pauline applied to the Carmel of Lisieux and, undoubtedly putting off a potentially traumatic announcement, did not immediately share the news with Thérèse, who learned the truth when she overheard a conversation between Pauline and Marie. Her 'little mother,' her 'ideal,' would leave her to enter the cloister in October of that year.

'In one instant, I understood what life was; until then I had never seen it so sad; but it appeared to me in all its reality, and I saw it was nothing but a continual suffering and separation. . . . Having heard about it by surprise, it was as if a sword were buried in my heart.'

Truly, Pauline had fulfilled every hope Zélie might have voiced regarding the tutelage and care of Thérèse. She'd been devoted and dependable and affectionate, and she had unintentionally scripted any movement toward her own independence as a betrayal. Thérèse cherished and inflated her every word and even believed Pauline had promised her that one day the two of them would go together to a 'faraway desert place,' where they could be hermits, apart from the world, together before God: a fantastic happiness for Thérèse, union with her chosen mother, withdrawal from all threat of separation. Writing of the plan, the adult Thérèse could admit that it was indeed a fantasy, a pious version of playing house, 'no doubt not said seriously, but little Thérèse had taken it seriously.' In any case, it would have been impossible to overstate what was for her a profound and dangerous shock.

Nine years old, Thérèse regressed into piteous and servile clinging. As when she had returned to Alençon from her wet nurse in Semallé and held tight to Zélie's skirts, Thérèse couldn't let Pauline out of her sight. Every day she brought her older sister little gifts – cakes and sweets that would be forbidden once Pauline was inside the convent – and covered her 'little mother' with what can be interpreted only as petitionary kisses. What did she have, other than love, to save herself from abandonment?

Nothing, and Thérèse's was human love, the same emotion she dismissed in her careless friends as imperfect, inconstant, 'narrow.' In her turn, each Martin daughter, first Pauline, then Marie, Thérèse, Céline, and Léonie, would sacrifice human bonds for the hope of perfect – divine – love. On October 2, 1882, Pauline entered Carmel, or, from the perspective of her little sister and pupil, she left.

It is estimated that, at the time of Pauline's postulancy, seven of every thousand French women were nuns, compared with four on the eve of the Revolution, one hundred years earlier. The nineteenth-century splintering of a previously homogeneous Catholicism into various factions allowed women a more powerful presence in what had been a male-dominated faith. Vocations were at an all-time high and were heard loudest in the towns and small cities, dioceses such as Bayeux, which included Lisieux. Paris and rural regions filled far fewer convents than did the bourgs, with their more rigid social hierarchies.

For girls who did not marry – girls tainted by a family history of tuberculosis, marred by smallpox, or, like Zélie, girls whose dowries were spent on a brother's education – entering a religious order guaranteed a respectable role in life as well as a surrogate family and security in old age. 'A dynamic young woman from a Catholic and cultured home with drive and ambition could not do better than become a nun.' Contemporary readers might balk at the idea of a woman choosing to forsake sexual satisfaction, but in nineteenth-century France, what sex life was to be had outside the convent? When the Church was hostile to all earthly pleasures, especially those of the body, there were few sexually liberated married Catholics. A well-brought-up, catechized girl had never even heard of an orgasm.

The fastest-growing orders were *congréganistes* and service-oriented, drawing young women who might today become teachers, nurses, or social workers. Known as *bonnes soeurs,* they ministered to the sick and the destitute, they taught the children of the poor, they answered a complex of growing needs that the state had yet to address. In contrast, orders of *religieuses,* like the Carmelites, were cloistered and comparatively elitist. For each postulant they required a dowry of up to ten thousand francs, attracting daughters of the professional bourgeoisie to a strictly regulated life dedicated to contemplation and prayer, silence rather than engagement. The Lisieux Carmel was in the center of town on the rue de Livarot, its members housed in a two-story cloister built around a garden with an allée of chestnut trees. The buildings were of plain red brick, functional and solid rather than graceful. To the bereft nine-year-old, however, the neoclassical facade of the entry, its columns and pediment, would have seemed both imposing and majestic.

On the brilliantly clear fall day that Pauline went through the spiked iron gate separating convent from town, Thérèse, responding with the monomania typical of the bereaved, 'was astonished the sun was shining with such brightness' on so sad an occasion. To make things worse, she was forced that same Monday to return to the school she hated. And she had no opportunity to forge any psychic defense: every Thursday she was expected to accompany her family to the cloister, to visit with her sister on the other side of a grille.

'Perhaps, dear Mother,' she wrote Pauline twelve years later, 'you find I am exaggerating the pain I was experiencing?

I readily admit that it should not have been as great . . . but my soul was FAR from being mature.' A mature soul would have been a soul like Zélie's, a soul with a tested apparatus for converting earthly torments to spiritual advancement. But Thérèse was still a child and, as would become clear, she had been not merely wounded by her mother's unavoidable abandonments; she had been damaged.

Pauline introduced her little sister to the mother superior of the Lisieux Carmel, Marie de Gonzague, who was charmed by the girl's unusual piety and tried to comfort her with promises that she, too, could follow a vocation into Carmel. But what could assuage so profound a loss, one that recapitulated the agony of her mother's death, provoking grief and rage she had not been able to express five years earlier?

By the end of 1882, Thérèse was plagued by unremitting headaches and abdominal pains, and, even more ominously in the case of this child, her behavior deteriorated along with her health. She suffered conflicts with her soul mate Céline; she talked back to Marie, who tried to assume the role of her third mother.

For Holy Week of 1883, Louis made a trip to Paris with Marie and Léonie and left the younger girls to spend Easter vacation with Céline and Isidore Guérin and their two children. The many years of correspondence between the Martin girls and their aunt and uncle attest to an unusual devotion between the families. Clearly Thérèse and Céline depended especially on this second set of parents; their love and need were generously returned. Noting Thérèse's despondency during the Easter visit, her uncle took her on a walk, sharing his plans for amusing distractions and speaking, as Thérèse recalled, 'about Mama and about past memories with a kindness that touched me profoundly and made me cry.'

More than that, Uncle Isidore's implicit acknowledgment of what everyone else seemed determined to deny – that Thérèse's misery centered on Zélie – quickened the child's anguish into physical illness. For months, everyone had insisted that Thérèse remain stoic, that she attend school with her aching head and each week cheerfully visit the cause of her distress. Now that her uncle had recognized – and permitted – her grief, she succumbed to it entirely. Observing that Thérèse was in no condition to attend the Catholic social to which the family had been invited, her aunt put her to bed with piles of blankets and hot water bottles to ease the shivering brought on by hysteria. But by morning, Thérèse was no better.

According to the testimony of the Guérins' maid, Marcelline Husé, who attributed the girl's ailment to 'deep loneliness,' Thérèse was 'seized by nervous trembling, followed by attacks of fright and hallucinations several times a day.' Doctor Notta, the family physician (the same who had found Zélie's cancer inoperable), pronounced the illness 'very serious.' Louis Martin returned from Paris with Marie and Léonie; by all accounts Thérèse's life was in danger. But what was the disease? As interpreted by the Martin sisters during the beatification process, and as Thérèse herself wrote, it was the work of the devil, angered by Pauline's entry to Carmel and attacking a child destined to be a saint. A contemporary psychiatrist might suggest that it wasn't the devil but Thérèse who was furious, raging at having lost yet another mother.

Initially, she could not be moved from the Guérin house,

and her sister Marie stayed to nurse her until she could return to Les Buissonnets. Remarkably, in the middle of March, Thérèse was able, as she announced she would be, to attend the clothing ceremony of Pauline, to sit in the lap of her 'little mother,' now gratifyingly alarmed, to gather the kisses and prayers of the nuns of Carmel.

The next day, she relapsed. The following weeks were characterized by periods of violent agitation that gave way to long stupors during which Thérèse seemed insensible to those around her. When she could, she occupied herself by making petitionary wreaths of flowers for her altar to the Queen of Heaven. This was her sole amusement. Twenty years later, her sister Marie recounted 'terrifying dreams that depressed all who heard her cries of distress. Some nails fixed in the wall of the room suddenly became as thick, charred fingers to her, and she cried out, 'I'm afraid, I'm afraid!' Her eyes, usually so calm and so kindly, had a terror-stricken expression that is impossible to describe.' She was ill for two months with what Doctor Notta concluded was Saint Vitus's dance, or chorea, a nervous disorder that afflicts children, usually at the onset of puberty, and causes uncontrolled motor activity – jerks and grotesque spasms of the muscles.

But Thérèse's movements were not random. Consistently she was thrown or threw herself off the bed and onto the floor. Chorea, hysteria, diabolic possession? All of these, ultimately, are semantic differences. The patient herself was consumed by doubts. Others judged that she sank into comas, but as she remembered, 'I was not deprived of the use of my reason for one single instant.' She heard and later remembered all that was said at her bedside; more significant, she worried she 'had become ill on purpose,' a private anxiety that hints at the disease's genesis within her own desires – for punishment of her family and herself, for the opportunity to escape the remarkable, even injurious, self-control that had character-ized her from as young as three, when she sat quietly for hours during Céline's catechism, a self-possession that had suppressed and thwarted subsequent years of grief and anger.

In gestures that were inextricably both affectionate and cruel, Pauline sent Thérèse letters and prayers accompanied by the gifts of an hourglass – so she might see that time did in fact pass, or so she could measure the dreadful tedium of ill-ness? – and a doll dressed in the habit of a Carmelite, lest she escape for a moment the vision of her longing, and her tor-ment. 'Uncle wasn't too happy,' Thérèse reported of the reception of the doll, perhaps allowing Isidore Guérin's sane voice to express what she denied. 'That instead of making me think of Carmel, it would be better to remove it from my mind.' Doctor Notta prescribed hydrotherapy, but the pros-pect of disrobing for showers was too horrible to a girl who later admitted she was 'troubled at having a body . . . not at ease in it . . . ashamed of it.' Perhaps it's no accident that the trembling and agitation of chorea typically announce puberty's turmoil, the clamor of the flesh; but whatever name was given Thérèse's complaint, its resolution would be as abrupt and mysterious as its onset.

On May 13, 1883, Pentecost Sunday, Thérèse experienced a second, celebrated apparition. The day had begun badly, with the ten-year-old girl even more distressed and disoriented than usual. Marie was in the garden, Léonie watching by the bed, while Thérèse continued to call out 'Maman! Maman!' – a plea so relentless, so familiar, that no one paid attention. It wasn't until she began screaming that Marie came back inside and Céline ran into the sickroom as well. Marie offered Thérèse some water, and she 'cried out in terror, "They want to poison me!"' It was a hysterical cry, certainly, and yet one with explicit content; that Thérèse later insisted she never lost her reason makes it impossible to dismiss her choice of words as meaningless. Even if we resist forcing a literal gloss upon her accusation – 'poison' a metaphor of toxic despair, all she was expected to swallow rather than express – the Martin family's faith asked much of a child. When Zélie died, Thérèse had been taught to turn a face of sweet acceptance to an unappeasable God, one who had now taken Pauline and must have seemed intent on removing her every comfort. What was the cost of continuing to perceive that God as a good God, a God of love?

Thérèse thrashed and screamed, and her three sisters, frightened, knelt down and began praying to the statue of Our Lady of Victories, the same to which their mother had turned after the death of Hélène and which she had heard speaking words of reassurance. 'She is here by my side,' Zélie had heard the Virgin say, a story told over and over, a script, some might judge.

'Three times I repeated the same prayer,' Marie testified. 'At the third time, I saw Thérèse fix her gaze on the statue, radiantly, like one in ecstasy. She confided in me that she had seen the blessed Virgin herself. This vision lasted four or five minutes.'

A cure would have restored Thérèse to her previous self.

These few minutes transformed her. 'Beautiful to me, so beautiful,' she wrote years later. 'Her face was suffused with an ineffable benevolence and tenderness.' Immediately, Thérèse understood that the apparition was private, even a secret, and that if she told anyone of it, her 'happiness would then disappear.' But her sisters were watching her face; they knew that something had transpired and that whatever it was had effected a miraculous rescue. Thérèse was returned to them: lucid, smiling, relaxed.

They pressed her with questions. Marie, in particular, waited until the two were alone and then pushed her little sister to betray that instinctive reticence common to religious experience. After all the months of worry Thérèse had caused Marie, she felt she owed her something – everything. She had seen the Virgin, Thérèse told Marie, and Marie told Pauline, and Pauline told the sisters of Carmel, and the child, soon well enough to visit the convent, was questioned closely. What was the Virgin wearing? Had she said anything? Was she carrying the Infant Jesus? Immediately, Thérèse's experience was appropriated by others eager for a vicarious glimpse of heaven.

The cult of the Virgin was never more powerful than in the nineteenth century, when many French girls, including the Martins, joined a religious society called the Children of Mary, whose pious exercises were a means to secure the chastity of adolescents. Invoked by countless young women to comfort and protect them, the Virgin appeared to Catherine Labouré in Paris in 1830, to Mélanie Mathieu in La Salette in 1846, and to Bernadette Soubirous in Lourdes in 1858. Such visions, Bernadette's in particular, were exhaustively publicized and contributed to a climate of expectation among French Catholics. 'A lady, young and beautiful, exceedingly beautiful, the like of whom I had never seen, came and placed herself at the entrance of the opening above the rosebush. She looked at me . . . smiled at me . . . as if she had been my mother.' Thus Bernadette described an experience very like Thérèse's. Fourteen in 1858, Bernadette was still living in 1877 when Zélie made her pilgrimage to Lourdes, where a witness to the young shepherdess's transports told Madame Martin of the indelible experience. The Virgin appeared to Bernadette eighteen times. She recited the rosary with the girl, she taught her a prayer (which Bernadette never shared), and she gave instructions for the building of a chapel. Bernadette's ecstasies were witnessed by friends, townspeople, and later clergy, and while those others saw nothing, the girl was able to describe the Virgin's yoked and pleated dress in detail, her blue ribbon and the white beads of her rosary, the yellow rose shining on each of her bare feet.

Thérèse, alas, could not provide any such details. 'Seeing that the Carmelites had imagined something else entirely, I thought I had lied,' she recalled, and the experience became a 'real spiritual trial for the next four years.' Having doubted the validity of her illness, now she doubted what restored her to health. As she said, 'I was unable to look upon myself without a feeling of profound horror,' a secret shame exacerbated by the solicitous affections of Marie de Gonzague, the prioress of Carmel. Mother Marie was fascinated by the little sister of her new novice: impressed by Thérèse's piety, worried by her endangered health, riveted by the report of the apparition. 'Mother Marie de Gonzague kisses her dear little daughter,' read a typical postscript to one of Pauline's letters home. Would it be possible to overstress how Thérèse cherished these tokens and how miserable she was to think she might not truly merit the indulgences of this august woman – a surrogate with heaven's stamp of approval, a mother who was already encouraging her to think seriously of a religious vocation?

Thérèse had not been dishonest, but she couldn't answer a question that persists: Was the experience one of neurosis or of supernatural revelation? And this, in turn, is a question that has validity only to those who admit the possibility of the second. Does the one necessarily exclude the other? Is anguish blind to the divine? Or perhaps might it sometimes be granted extra powers of perception?

Just as the sight of her stooped and aged father bore witness to her fears over his mortality as much as to any divine communication, Thérèse's miracle was personal and private; it unfolded only for the child who experienced it. Whether this means it *issued from* or *was delivered to* her psyche is a question without a single answer. The atheist sees a neurotic symptom, the believer the grace of God, and the biographer a leap of creativity, one that testifies as much to Thérèse's resilience as to the damage she suffered.

In any case, in the wake of devastating loss, Thérèse was given, or she gave herself, a vision of a mother who would never leave her.

AFTER HER CURE, and before her return to the dreaded Benedictine school, Louis took Thérèse on a trip to Alençon. It was the first time she'd visited the town where she was born and where her mother had died, and she welcomed the chance to pray at Zélie's grave and ask for her dead mother's protection as the visit's highlight. Ten years old, quaint and awkward and solemn, she regarded this time in Alençon as her 'first entrance into the world.' She was spoiled, she was petted and admired and entertained, and she found herself beguiled. 'The friends we had there were too worldly,' she would later judge, 'they knew too well how to ally the joys of this earth to the service of God.' In other words, what another might praise as balance, Thérèse rejected as lacking in piety. 'They didn't think about death enough.'

With Louis as chaperone, it's hard to imagine that Thérèse's entertainments were anything but modest and provincial, undeserving of her suggestion of licentiousness. But saints don't become saints by choosing paths of moderation or tolerance. Increasingly, Thérèse inhabited a stark and fantastic landscape. She had seen beauty, a terrible and demanding beauty, one of the faces of God. Ecstasies are unforgettable, and they are tyrannical. Those who experience them helplessly shape their lives in order to create the possibility of another encounter with the holy. What sacrifice would be too great? At the end of her life, Thérèse dedicated a poem to Christ, whom she called her 'Supreme Beauty.' 'For you, I must die,' she exulted. Anything that separated her from God – her very life, her flesh – was to be obliterated.

For now, in the wake of the Virgin's apparition and the scrutiny it inspired, Thérèse became intensely self-conscious. Every material pleasure presented the problem of corruption. Nothing could be enjoyed without analyzing its potential spiritual tariff.

In retrospect, writing as a twenty-two-year-old bride of Christ, she dismissed the holiday in Alençon as a temptation: Jesus showed her the world she might have, were she to refuse his hand. The secular beckoned, it dazzled enough that she was threatened by her attraction to it, but it was impermanent and couldn't compare with the promise of heaven, of ultimate and lasting reunion with her mother and with God, the two barely distinguishable.

From behind the walls of Carmel, Pauline continued to guide her promising pupil, preparing Thérèse for her first communion. She made Thérèse a little book to fill each night with the day's 'flowers,' a more sophisticated tallying of spiritual progress than beads on a string. At the beatification process, Pauline testified that in the space of three months Thérèse made and recorded '818 sacrifices and 2,773 acts of love or aspirations' (a daily average of 9 sacrifices and 31 acts of love).

As for prayer, 'God was already instructing [her] in secret.' When one of the nuns at the abbey school asked Thérèse what she did with her free time, she answered that she hid herself between her bed and the wall, she pulled the curtain around her, and she thought. About what, the nun wanted to know: "about God, about life, about eternity . . . I think!' The good religious laughed heartily at me.' The teacher would continue to tease Thérèse about her answer. Even in the pious and edifying atmosphere of a convent school, she was an eccentric. She went on retreat to prepare for her communion and found the experience 'sweet,' remembering the sister who came to her in her dormitory bed to kiss her good night. Overwhelmed by what another child might have found a perfunctory morsel of affection, Thérèse withdrew the 'precious little book' of sacrifices from under her pillow, revealing her secret work, her 'eyes bright with joy.'

Thérèse was eleven years old, but she had never before dressed herself; she didn't know how to comb her own hair and had to ask for help from a nun who pulled, and she dared not cry as she did 'every day' under the more gentle hands of her sister Marie. Her father, along with Marie and Léonie, visited her each day of the retreat, presumably compromising the intent of such an exercise; Louis brought Thérèse cakes and treats she might otherwise miss. Away from home for the first time, Thérèse became aware that she had been 'fondled and cared for like few other children on earth.' Spoiled, certainly, but what child allows herself to grow to eleven without even token autonomy? Peculiarly dependent and passive, unaware of even the smallest expeditions into adulthood that other children prize, she 'made a spectacle' of herself by wearing a huge crucifix tucked, missionary fashion, into her belt.

Having suffered the well-intentioned trampling of her vision of Mary, she implied that her account of her first communion was not complete. 'I don't want to enter into detail here,' she explained in *Story of a Soul*, but she wrote that the confession she made filled her with peace and that she received her first communion as 'a kiss of love. I felt that I was loved, and I said: I love you and I give myself to you forever.' These words strike modern readers as overheated, but the emotion was not untypical of French Catholic girls of the period, who prepared for this rite of passage with great seriousness. Dressed and veiled as brides, souls freshly bleached by the confessional, they were encouraged to identify the rite as a type of marriage and earnestly awaited the arrival of their Holy Bridegroom. Transported by joy, Thérèse cried 'copious tears' during the mass; classmates assumed that she was missing her dead mother and absent sister. One, who overheard her prayers for death, tattled to the nun in charge.

At the celebratory family dinner, attended by all her sisters save Pauline, as well as by the Guérins, Thérèse's father gave her a gold watch he had made. She felt 'great pleasure,' but reflected that 'the gifts [she] received did not satisfy [her] heart.' All she wanted was Jesus, another opportunity to consume and be consumed by God. At eleven years old, her identity was that of a tormented lover, waiting from one communion – one meeting – to the next. And she knew of only one way to reach the object of her intensifying desire. 'Suffering became my attraction,' she confessed. 'It had charms about it which ravished me without my understanding them very well.'

Thérèse remained in the abbey school, having secured her own odd niche, continuing to preside like a miniature cleric over her 'very beautiful' cemetery for birds. 'Planted with trees and flowers in proportion to the size of our little feathered friends,' it was a kind of bookend to the aviary she kept at home. Birds would figure heavily in her poems, her mystical writing; in their variety they would represent the differences, and the commonality, of souls. She told stories, probably inspired by those she liked to read, books she consumed with a voraciousness she didn't allow herself to express elsewhere, 'tales of chivalry . . . accounts of French heroines, especially Joan of Arc.' Her classmates gathered around her to listen. Attentive to what pleased her audience, watching carefully the expressions on their faces, unconsciously practicing for the great work that would define her life, she strung the narratives out for days, collecting a larger and larger crowd until the nuns put an end to the entertainment, considering it more healthful for girls to run and play.

In May of 1885, when she was twelve, Thérèse went on a second retreat and, after a tranquil year, was 'assailed by the terrible sickness of scruples,' a torturous intensification of her moral consciousness that would persist for another eighteen months. Now it was no longer the environment that had to be assessed, but the girl. Thérèse subjected her every action and thought to examination and worry. Was it a sin and, if so, how serious? Her sister Marie offered the solace of a confessional ear, but the calming effect lasted no longer than the confession, the subject of which was often the scruples themselves. Was her intense self-consciousness, her sense of corruption, even dirtiness, brought on by puberty? It's hard not to wonder if Thérèse hadn't inadequately repressed a sexual awakening, especially as her account of her writhing anxiety is superimposed on an oedipal passage about her hair: 'For every day, to please Papa, the little Queen had her hair curled, to the surprise of her companions and especially her teachers.' So ready to fault herself for vanity, to repudiate something as small as a pretty ribbon, Thérèse betrayed no awareness of the irony of having her hair dressed so elaborately that it surprised her schoolmates, even as she 'did not stop crying while telling all my scruples.' Marie brushed and curled and listened; Thérèse confessed and wept.

At the end of the year, Céline left the abbey school and Thérèse found herself alone, without the company of someone who understood her. Severe headaches returned and her father, determined to avoid another complete breakdown, removed Thérèse from the abbey school and engaged a private teacher, Madame Papinau, whose sitting-room classes encouraged the conflict between spiritual and worldly grooming to smolder. Thérèse couldn't have learned much, because Madame's very convivial mother sat in the same parlor; a stream of guests came to call; and lessons were often interrupted by conversation and by admiring comments about her long golden curls and gray eyes, her nice clothes and good figure. Thérèse was thirteen. She wanted God, but she also wanted what all girls want: to be desired. To be desirable on mortal terms. Throughout her *Story of a Soul,* she dismissed compliments, she judged them of little value, but she didn't fail to report them.

Marie guided Thérèse through the trial of scruples. Probably exasperated by what she later identified as her little sister's 'so-called sins,' she tried suggesting to Thérèse that she would take them onto her own soul and concluded by limiting the number of faults she would allow Thérèse to confess. Grateful for the help – she knew she needed it – Thérèse would clearly have preferred Pauline. 'Finally I ended up by recognizing the sad reality: Pauline is lost to me,' she would write in her autobiography, 'almost in the same manner as if she were dead.' Very much in the same manner, if readers pause to remember how Thérèse defined death: like Zélie, Pauline had abandoned Thérèse to enter into a closer communion with God.

This acknowledgment of loss gave way to its natural, or at least expectable, result: a private cult of mourning and worship. In the attic room where Pauline used to paint, Thérèse made a retreat for herself, and she described its charms with even greater devotion and idolatry than she had the altar over which she'd fought with Victoire. Again, it was a space minutely and deliberately 'arranged to suit [her] taste,' but six years had passed, and Thérèse's ability to create an atmosphere of religious longing had evolved. The attic included plants, candles, flowers, baskets made of shells, a cage filled with birds, a cross, a statue of the Virgin, likenesses of the saints – in sum, an ornate shrine, at the center of which was 'enthroned all by itself the portrait of Pauline.'

In September of 1885, Thérèse and Céline went to Trouville

for a seaside holiday with the Guérins while their father was in Constantinople. Happy at the beach, Thérèse rode a donkey, fished for eels, and took so much delight in some blue hair ribbons that she felt constrained to report her vanity in the confessional. Observing that her cousin Marie was pampered when she complained of headaches, Thérèse, whose head ached all the time, imitated her. But the experiment went amiss; everyone was so used to Thérèse's stoicism that they assumed she could not be whimpering over pain as trifling as a headache, and they scolded her for lying. Thérèse reported that she was 'cured for life' of any desire to attract attention.

Always prone to homesickness, she was glad to return to Les Buissonnets, to the attic shrine, where she spent hours meditating on the view, the town, taking great pleasure in her solitude and in her aviary with its most recent addition, a linnet, prized for its song. But when she learned that Marie was going to enter Carmel, the room abruptly 'lost its attraction.'

Once again, Thérèse regressed miserably; she couldn't pass by Marie's door without knocking and entering, without making obeisance in the form of kisses and tears. In September of 1886, a month before his eldest daughter was to enter the cloister, Louis took Marie, as well as Thérèse and Céline, on a farewell visit to Alençon, where Thérèse admitted that she 'made a big fuss over everything,' especially over having forgotten to bring a bouquet of flowers she'd gathered for Zélie's grave, a critical gesture in the worship, the supplication, of Mother. Looking back, years past the wretchedness of adolescence, she didn't even recognize herself in the tormented thirteen-year-old who couldn't stop crying, a girl so out of control that she 'caused certain people in Alençon to say [she] had a weak character.'

If Thérèse's histrionics were an unconscious means of redirecting attention from Marie back to herself, the Martins returned to Lisieux having discovered that it was not only Thérèse who was bent on upstaging her older sister. Without warning, without so much as saying good-bye, Léonie had made her first attempt to join the Poor Clares in Alençon. Marie was furious, and everyone was embarrassed and bewildered by Léonie's secrecy. The family visited the monastery on the rue Demi-Lune, and Thérèse described both the buildings and its inhabitants as oddly repellent, a feeling that seems to have mystified her, even as it was in keeping with the Martins' habitual censure of the middle sister. Léonie told her family to get a good look at her eyes, which she would henceforth have to 'guard,' or keep modestly trained on the ground. But, as Thérèse wrote, somewhat disingenuously, after two months Léonie came home 'to show us her blue eyes which were frequently moist with tears,' her skin broken by eczema, a condition often exacerbated by strain.

On October 15, 1886, Marie entered Carmel, and Thérèse was left to battle her scruples alone. Lacking mortal advisers, she followed the example of Zélie and prayed to her dead brothers and sisters, introducing herself as the youngest and most petted child and telling them she expected solace for one who was, after all, their sister.

VERY EARLY on Christmas morning 1886, during 'that luminous night which sheds such light,' Thérèse Martin came home from midnight mass with her father and Céline. As was the custom for French children, she had left her shoes on the hearth, empty in anticipation of gifts, not from Father Christmas but from the Child Jesus, who was imagined to travel through the air bearing toys and cakes. Perhaps Monsieur Martin was exhausted by the hour – he was not young, and the sight of the expectant shoes would have been yet another reminder of the relentless emotional demands of his weepy youngest daughter.

'Thank goodness this will be the last year!' Thérèse heard him say as she was going up the stairs to put away her coat, words spoken with such uncharacteristic annoyance that Thérèse would credit Jesus with their suggestion. Whether the words were divinely inspired or not, had her father known she could hear him, he would probably have remained silent, would never have spoken such words which, like a spell, 'pierced my heart.'

Who else's displeasure could have struck so deeply? Father was everything to this teenager; he was the one who had never abandoned her; he was the focus of her romantic love, her King and her savior. As she would write in her 'Canticle of Céline,' an 1895 poem about the warmth and joy of family: 'How I loved receiving my father's caresses, / Gazing upon his hair / White and snowy . . . / Sitting on his lap / I remember being rocked for a long time.' The whiff of sexual feeling (projected onto her sister) is sanitized by Thérèse's identifying her father with Christ, the lover who 'virginizes,' to use a verb of her own coinage. From another poem, written a year later: 'When I love Christ and when I touch him / My heart becomes purer, I am even more chaste. / The kiss of his mouth has given me the treasure / Of virginity.'

Censure from that mouth was unbearable, and thus transformative.

Upon hearing her father's sharp remark, Thérèse began to cry, and Céline, always hoping to avoid extra upset, tried to prevent her from going back downstairs to the hearth, to the ruined ritual of opening her little gifts. But Thérèse 'was no longer the same.' In an instant she had been elevated from needy child to loving adult. She dried her face; she ran downstairs; in front of her beloved father she took her 'magic shoes,' unwrapped and exclaimed over each gift 'with the happy appearance of a Queen. Having regained his own cheerfulness,' her father laughed with her. On the face of it, this early Christmas morning of 1886 was the same as those of years previous, and yet Thérèse understood that she had been remade.

Céline, who had endured countless scenes and daily, sometimes hourly, tears, was frankly shocked. During the beatification process, her sister and close confidante testified that Thérèse had transcended in an instant 'a period of darkness' that had begun ten years before, at the death of their mother. Previously, as Thérèse said, she had been excessively shy and sensitive, she had 'practiced virtue without feeling the sweetness of it.' This was a great understatement: she had been consumed by obsessive worries about sin. 'For the first time,' Céline said, 'I saw her completely control herself in a disappointment that would previously have left her desolate.'

To mortal appearance, she mastered herself at long last, but Thérèse did not understand the event by mortal, secular measure. She knew she had been given a great grace, that of 'complete conversion.' After all, in the past she *had* tried to control herself, had tried with all her being and had failed. Now she did not have to try. 'On that night of light began the third period of my life, the most beautiful and the most filled with graces from heaven.'

Denied a magic given to children, Thérèse Martin found – she was given – a different and transcendent power. She would still suffer, but she would no longer grieve; she was flooded with 'charity . . . the need to forget [her]self and to please others.'

Grace, alchemy, masochism: through whatever lens we view her transport, Thérèse's night of illumination presented both its power and its danger. It would guide her steps between the mortal and the divine, between living and dying, destruction and apotheosis. It would take her exactly where she intended to go.

*

Soon after Christmas, Thérèse was looking at a picture of Jesus' crucifixion. She liked religious art; many of her metaphors, and her epiphanies, issued from paintings. 'Struck by the blood flowing from one of the divine hands,' she was overcome by the idea of its falling without being caught. She determined that her place would be at the foot of the cross, gathering the blood of Christ, the blood of salvation, and in her turn pouring it out. She 'burned with the desire to snatch [sinners] from the eternal flames.'

An opportunity presented itself in the form of Henri Pranzini, a criminal celebrated and reviled in the kind of tabloid newspapers Louis Martin never allowed his daughters to read. But the demimonde case had seized the imagination of everyone, especially the citizens of the provincial town. Women were scandalized and thrilled by Pranzini's murder of Régine de Montelle – a Parisienne of the type Louis Martin feared and abhorred from his student days: sexual, amoral, and beautiful – as well as her maid and de Montelle's twelve-year-old daughter. The murderer was described as a 'tall and handsome adventurer,' unrepentant even when condemned, on July 13, to death.

In what seems a triumph of sexual repression, Thérèse chose Pranzini as her 'first child,' the name she would henceforth give to the dangerous male predator with whom she began her lifelong mission of substitutive suffering. Perhaps, in that he sacrificed both mother and daughter, never rupturing their bond but instead dispatching the two to heaven together, Pranzini struck Thérèse as a sympathetic brand of killer. With Céline she prayed and made sacrifices for his conversion, for God's pardon, for his escape from the fires of hell. And she asked for a sign that her prayers would be answered. On August 31, 1887, Pranzini was guillotined. At the last moment he seized the crucifix offered him and 'kissed the sacred wounds three times,' a scene that Thérèse read about in *La Croix*, the Catholic royalist newspaper to which her father subscribed, and that she remembered and reported in voluptuous detail in her *Story of a Soul*.

Thérèse's account of the Pranzini case is immediately followed by her judging herself to have been during this period 'at the most dangerous age for young girls,' an oblique reference to sexual awakening. Neither Thérèse nor any of her sisters ever alluded to physical desire in any but the most vague and sanitized language, but her meaning is clear; and this textual juxtaposition is similar to the earlier one that paired her description of weeping over her inescapable feelings of corruption with that of having her hair dressed. To save her from the looming possibility of carnal sin, Thérèse reported, Jesus chose this moment to take her for his own. Pranzini's kissing the crucifix had shown her that her petitions were heard; now, as Thérèse described it, Christ washed her with precious perfumes, he reclothed her in embroidered robes, he gave her priceless ornaments and made her his queen.

The implicit sexuality of these images, chosen not at fourteen but at twenty-one, strikes a secular audience more forcefully than it does readers of hagiography. The language of sexual love, of ravishing and abandonment, is the language of the saints as much as it is the libertine's. Human love, be it chaste or consummated, has limited expression.

*

As always, avoiding provocative books – 'Never did God permit me to read a single one of them that was capable of doing me any harm' – Thérèse steeped herself in her favorite works, *The Imitation of Christ* by Thomas à Kempis, and *End of the Present World and the Mysteries of the Life to Come* by Abbé Arminjon, from whom she took the idea that mortal life is analogous to an ocean voyage: a means from here to there, temporary, the body a ship soon left behind. What she found in these books was not information so much as confirmation of all she had learned as a child of Zélie and Louis Martin: the joys and tribulations of the present world counted for nothing. All that mattered was preparing for the next life.

Thérèse confided to Céline what she waited until Pentecost Sunday 1887 to tell her father: she intended to enter Carmel, as soon as possible. As she remembered it, her 'dear Céline did not rebel for one instant,' either at the idea of Thérèse's entering out of turn or at the prospect of being left, at eighteen, to cope with their father's old age, a trial that would fall on Céline more heavily than either of them could guess (and one that Léonie would largely avoid, caught as she was in her own struggles).

As for Louis Martin, already he had suffered the losses of Pauline and Marie. He would never withhold a sacrifice asked him by God, but it had cost him dearly to part with his elder daughters, and as everyone acknowledged, Thérèse was his favorite, his own Little Queen before she was Jesus'.

While much of Thérèse's language – her 'flowers' and her 'toys,' her 'little birds' and 'sweet tears flowing' – cloaks a fierce and uncompromising nature, the occasional uncensored slip testifies to the sway she held over her family, to her arrogance and her awareness, at least in retrospect, that she had set herself against whoever might oppose the vocation of a fourteen-year-old; and there would be a long list. If Céline did not *rebel*, others would. Thérèse prayed to the apostles to inspire her with the right words to speak to her father, but she was asking his blessing, not his permission.

She found him in the garden of Les Buissonnets, the scene of her altars and games, and at the sight of his 'handsome face,' its 'heavenly expression,' she was filled with peace. What chance did so docile and self-sacrificing a 'dear little father' have against her will, formidable by itself, now wedded to God's? She began to cry and Louis asked the cause for her tears. 'He didn't say one word to turn me. . . . I defended myself so well.' Louis, along with Céline, was scripted as a possible adversary, his 'dearness' dependent upon his passivity.

Monsieur Martin pulled a 'little white flower' from beside a low wall and gave it to Thérèse as a symbol of herself, who had bloomed in a protected garden, who had ripened in purity to be plucked by God. The flower came up roots and all, and Thérèse kept it as a relic, 'destined to live on in another soil more fertile.' Two years before her death, when she wrote of the experience, she noted that the roots had broken off, a sign that God would soon be severing the earthly bonds of his little flower.

Having recently suffered the first in a series of strokes, an aged and frail Louis Martin did not oppose Thérèse. Her uncle Isidore, however, found the idea of a fourteen-year-old nun preposterous: the whole town would be scandalized.

Canon Delatroëtte, the ecclesiastical superior of Carmel, insisted she wait until she was twenty-one. The prioress, Mother Marie de Gonzague, as well as her sister Marie, sided with Delatroëtte. Bishop Hugonin of Bayeux, for whom Thérèse put up her hair in the hope that it might make her look older, refused to override the local authority. Thérèse's last resort was none other than the pope.

On November 4, 1887, Louis Martin, Céline, and Thérèse embarked on a pilgrimage, in many ways a typical grand tour of Europe, but one led by a vicar general, Father Révérony, culminating in an audience with Pope Leo XIII. The Martins traveled among a party of priests and Catholic royalists, whose ability to enjoy worldly luxuries en route to a celebration of Leo's jubilee both threatened and disgusted Thérèse. What she didn't know was that even before the travelers left home, the spiritual dimension of the trip had been eclipsed by its political agenda. French bishops were dispatching bands of pilgrims to Rome as a means of declaring loyalty to a Vatican that France had failed to protect from the unification of Italy. (In 1870, when the French garrison pulled out of Rome because troops were needed to protect the homeland from an invading Prussian army, the last of the papal domains were annexed to the Italian state.) The humiliating French defeat by the Prussians and the subsequent birth (in 1871) of the Third Republic had marked a decline of the conservative right's power. Forced onto the defensive, the royalist bourgeoisie perceived a strong Church as an important means of safeguarding France's integrity and its future. As the granddaughter of two career soldiers, Thérèse was heir to a development she did not at all perceive: the rise of a militant nationalist Catholicism, a trend that would, in 1894, result in the anti-Semitic scapegoating and trumped-up treason conviction of a young army captain named Alfred Dreyfus.

Still a sheltered child, Thérèse lived in ignorance of political events and motivations; and she had never before had the opportunity to observe priests in a casual context. Finding them all too human, she conceived a lifelong ambition to pray especially for those mortals entrusted with the care of other souls, a petition she understood as economical, a way of reaching many for the price of one.

Worried beforehand about the possibility of inadvertently looking at indiscreet paintings or sculpture, art that revealed genitalia, Thérèse 'commended her purity to St. Joseph' and found herself safe from corruption. If there was anything to see, she missed it. During the trip she mingled with young men for the first time, one of whom was attracted to her, and she to him – enough that she observed in private to Céline that hers was a heart that 'could easily be captured by affection,' an attachment that would cause her to 'perish,' as she had no means to defend herself against the weakness of mortal love. But 'God's great mercy preserved' her.

Always awed by nature, in which she could take pleasure even as she praised God's bounty, Thérèse loved Switzerland, and when the train crossed through the Alps, she 'ran from one side of the carriage to the other,' very much a teenager, excited to be alive. In Bologna, jostled and carried across a street by an Italian student, she dispatched the provocative young man with a look of disapproval. Venice was 'sad' but offered the occasion to fantasize about martyrs, as did the other Italian cities they visited, her most ardent flights reserved for Rome. Like the provincial French girl she was, Thérèse praised the holy city's center as a place 'where one could easily believe one was in Paris, judging by the magnificence of the hotels and stores.' But it was the Colosseum that transported her, that arena of blood spilled in the name of Christ. Initially disappointed by the 'heap of ruins' that seemed to mock the splendor of her fantasies, with her usual sense of entitlement – permission granted by God – Thérèse persuaded Céline to scramble with her past a barrier and down a stepladder, where the 'two fugitives,' deaf to their father's calls, threw themselves on the 'sacred dust,' kissed it, and gathered stones to carry home. In the catacombs, the fervent grave robbers – 'we had to carry off some souvenir' – took away earth from the tomb of Saint Cecilia, whom Thérèse subsequently adopted as 'intimate confidante. Everything in her thrilled me, especially her abandonment, her limitless confidence.'

She plundered the tomb of Saint Agnes for a mosaic chip to bring home to Pauline, whose vocational name was Agnes of Jesus. She spent six feverish days in the holy city gobbling experiences, it would seem, against the coming privations of the cloister.

She who repudiated the body, who found eating so shameful that she considered it 'something you ought to go aside to do,' implicitly equating meals with neither pleasure nor sustenance but with their excretory destiny, enjoyed the food in Italy so much that years later, dying in the cloister and suffering the fantasies of the starving, she remembered those sumptuous repasts and, to her humiliation, was overcome with desire for them.

On her seventh day in Rome, a day 'both longed for and dreaded,' Thérèse saw the pope. Sunday, November 20, began with a heavy rainfall, which, with characteristic monomania, Thérèse could interpret only as an inauspicious portent. After celebrating a mass of thanksgiving in the Vatican's papal chapel, Leo XIII sat on a raised armchair in his audience room, where he was surrounded by defensive ranks of cardinals and archbishops. Papal audiences were not unusual – the Vatican was a fashionable destination, His Holiness's blessing something of a status symbol – but they were strictly orchestrated. The pilgrims, dressed in black, women with their heads covered (in accordance with Vatican rule), passed before His Holiness in turn. As instructed, each knelt, kissed his foot and his hand, and received his benediction. Thérèse had been warned that it was absolutely forbidden to address the pontiff. Still, instead of kissing his hand, she put hers together in prayer and told Leo XIII that she had a favor to ask him. In honor of his jubilee, would he permit her to enter Carmel at fifteen? Confused, Leo turned Révérony for explanation, and the vicar explained that the superiors in Bayeux were considering the matter.

'Oh Holy Father, if you say yes,' Thérèse pressed, 'everyone will agree!'

'Go. Go,' the pope said. 'You will enter if God wills it.' Thérèse was dragged away from his feet.

'Two guards touched me politely to make me rise,' she would recall. 'As this was not enough, they took me by the arms and Father Révérony helped them to lift me, for I stayed there with joined hands resting on the knees of Leo XIII.' Having done all she could for herself, Thérèse would have to wait, in hope and faith. She felt peace 'at the bottom of [her] heart.' Bitterness, grief, and impatience filled the rest of her.

The French Catholic publication *L'Univers* reported on the pilgrims' reception and on 'a young girl of fifteen who begged the Holy Father for permission to enter a convent immediately. . . . His Holiness encouraged her to be patient, to pray very much, and to seek counsel from God and her conscience. This caused the young girl to break down into sobs.'

There remained only the solace of visits to tombs and reliquaries, where, Thérèse reflected, she 'always had to find a way of touching everything.' In Rome's Church of the Holy Cross, she managed to insinuate her littlest finger into a golden casket bearing a 'nail bathed in the blood of Jesus.' In Florence, hers was the only arm small enough to fit through the grille of the Carmelite choir and touch the relics of Magdalen de' Pazzi. Saint Magdalen's was a life that Thérèse would have embraced as exemplary. A child of unnaturally strong will, Magdalen had thwarted her mother, outperformed her in piety to enter the cloister at sixteen and follow what Rudolph Bell has described as 'a well-established path of religious expression for women,' the major theme of which was suffering. 'Visited by God with strange painful maladies' as she evolved spiritually toward the consummation of death, the heavenly arms of the Bridegroom, Magdalen refused food, whipped herself, pierced her flesh with thorns and spikes, and finally succumbed in 1607 to an illness marked by chest pains, fever, and coughing.

In Florence, in 1887, the other pilgrims passed their rosaries to Thérèse, who enjoyed the privilege of obtaining their sanctification, pressing them against the relics of the baroquely masochistic Saint Magdalen. Always transported by stories of martyrdom, by the romance of death, Thérèse greedily gathered in such narratives, even as she was gathered in by them.

She admitted that she was brazen in her desire, her need to commune with any and every available trace of God's presence. Like a lover fondling a shorn lock of hair, a billet-doux, she pursued the rapture she'd tasted. Motherless, petted and indulged to compensate for grievous loss, she presumed God would always understand her as 'a child who believes everything is permitted.'

And perhaps she was not far wrong. Having expressed disapproval of Thérèse's premature vocation, Father Révérony had an unexpected change of heart in the wake of her disobedience. Was it her determination, strong enough to lead her to thwart Vatican officials, that convinced him of her sincerity? In the course of the return journey, he promised her to 'do all he could' to facilitate her entrance to Carmel.

THÉRÈSE RETURNED to Lisieux on December 2, 1887. In her absence, her sister Pauline had been writing letters on her behalf and working, successfully, to convince Mother Marie de Gonzague that Thérèse was mature beyond her years and that three Martin sisters in the same convent would not constitute a lobby within the community's inescapably insular politics. Her uncle Isidore moved from resignation to advocacy and met with the unmovable Delatroëtte, who, sensing conspiracy, accused the prioress of acting 'underhandedly.'

With the help of her uncle and the collaboration of Pauline and Mother Marie, Thérèse drafted and redrafted a letter to the bishop, reminding him of her ardor. Whatever fears she had, she did not express: 'I believe it is through you that Jesus is going to carry out his promise,' she wrote. Why would God call her so insistently if He were not ultimately to welcome her into Carmel? Stubbornly, she held the hope of celebrating the first anniversary of her conversion with the gift of the bishop's acquiescence. But in contrast to the previous year's epiphany, this Christmas came and went without word.

On December 28, the prioress received a letter from Bishop Hugonin: she could decide herself whether to admit Thérèse.

On New Year's Day, the eve of her fifteenth birthday, Thérèse visited Pauline at the Carmel and was told she had been accepted as a postulant but, in a pragmatic concession to her youth and her frail constitution, her entrance would be postponed until after Lent, a 'three months exile,' as Thérèse saw it, not to spare but to deny her the rigors of fasting, of spending winter in an unheated building. Mother Marie de Gonzague was in no hurry. Thérèse was just fifteen; what good could come of breaking her spirit or her health? Besides, a delay would be at least a small concession to Delatroëtte; it would give the angry canon a chance to cool off.

Thérèse was indeed fifteen, impatient as only a teenager can be. Three months was a torturous postponement, a sacrifice of such magnitude that she could take pride in providing this worthy dowry of suffering. Letters she received from Pauline while she waited to hear from the bishop and the prioress introduced the theme of the Child Jesus' toy: Thérèse was a ball, a humble amusement for the Christ Child, who tossed it this way and that, who played with it and then forgot it. In the memorably suggestive words of her 'little mother,' Christ said, 'Never has My little ball given me so much pleasure, never; I have already pierced it several times . . . today I made a bigger hole. . . . Presently I am going to repair it, and this is how I'm going to do it! I am going to take it into My two little hands and blow very hard into it . . . place a kiss on the hole I have made. . . . How I love my little ball! I can pierce it; I can do all I

75

want with it and it always repeats, 'Jesus, I love you!''

Much as the image disturbs contemporary readers, who cannot free themselves from post-Freudian suspicion – an interpretation of piercing and blowing and kissing the rent ball as necessarily sexual – the idea of herself as a toy of Christ struck Thérèse as a perfectly innocent symbol, one that would ultimately become an integral part of her theology. To explain mortal trials as proceeding from infantile, if holy, caprice might seem cruel to those who cherish the idea of a reasonable God. Thérèse received the idea as a comfort, and the ball appears in nineteen letters between her and her family, as well as in three from her confessor, Père Pichon. It is mentioned in her autobiography; no doubt she later used it when instructing her novices. Typical of the excessive sentiment for which Thérèse is often faulted, the abused ball was as much a product of the era as of the girl. The Theresian scholar and translator John Clarke traces it to a leaflet given the young pilgrim at the Carmel before she embarked on her journey to Rome. Inspired by the image herself, and knowing its value to her sister, Céline had given Thérèse for Christmas a little boat she had made, inside of which was a figure of the sleeping Christ Child, holding his little ball. The name of the vessel, floating in a bowl of water, was *Self-Abandonment*.

Girding herself with visions of a love that wounds, that defies mortal understanding if not the urge to allegory, Thérèse used her exile as spiritual test and opportunity; she would make herself an even more worthy fiancée. She began the long process of fashioning what she would come to think of as an ornate wedding dress, each stitch purchased with an act of penance, a gesture of love.

Impatient, she behaved with all the grace she could muster; she practiced the 'nothings' of self-censure, of putting others' desires before her own. Small sacrifices in themselves, these increments of humbling, of subduing, would increasingly constitute her program of spiritual advancement. In the end, when every inclination to self had been squelched, the combined nothings would add up to a monumental and heroic something: martyrdom.

Offered one last trip by her father, a pilgrimage with him to the Holy Land, Thérèse declined. She went each day for lessons from Madame Papinau, where another pupil would remember clearly his last sight of Thérèse before she entered the convent: 'I can still see her on the pavement, mechanically turning the point of her umbrella in the groove of one of the curb stones. She was wearing a green dress edged with astrakhan and frogged trimmings, and her hair was tied with a sky-blue ribbon.' Described as tall and robust, with a round face that belied her ascetic impulses, Thérèse looked every bit a cosseted daughter of the bourgeoisie.

Surely one of the attractions of Carmel was aesthetic. Well clothed, well fed, Thérèse spent her days in rooms stuffed with furniture and furbelows. The austerity of the convent, its bare cells and simple, whitewashed refectory, its stone hallways traveled by identically dressed women, silent except for the sweep of the habit, the hiss of rope sandals – all this presented a physical grace and order that materialism had buried. At fifteen, an age that seeks a new language, a separate identity, Thérèse must have longed for bare stone floors underfoot as much as she did doctrine overhead.

On April 8, the Little Queen had a farewell dinner at home, at the heavy mahogany dining table of Les Buissonnets, surrounded by her father, her sisters Céline and Léonie (home from her second failed novitiate, this time as a Visitation nun), and the Guérins. The next morning, all attended mass together at the convent. Thérèse remembered that during the silence of communion she could hear 'nothing around me but sobs.' Thérèse didn't cry, but when she was summoned to the enclosure her 'heart was beating so violently it seemed impossible to walk' through the door separating the world from the cloister, freedom from service.

She knelt for her father's blessing, and he wept. The usually locked doors swung open and showed her the entire community assembled, black veils lowered over their faces. The outmaneuvered Canon Delatroëtte presented her to the prioress, absolving himself of any responsibility if 'this fifteen-year-old child' were to 'disappoint [her] hopes.' The cloister doors closed, and Thérèse followed her newest mother, Marie de Gonzague, into her new life.

The Carmel of Lisieux was a small and humble convent, even by the order's ascetic standards, and the physical privation of life within was compounded by a spirit of fear and penance. Their order having been founded in 1155, during the Latin occupation of Palestine, the Carmelites took their name from Mount Carmel, where the most extreme Crusaders eschewed the established and insufficiently severe religious societies to live as hermits in an enclave of tiny cells. For their spiritual father, they chose the prophet Elijah, who had hidden himself in the same mountain and 'whose word burned like a torch.' Guided by this soul for whom 'nothing was too hard,' the Carmelites gathered only for mass, devoting themselves to charity, to preaching, and above all to contemplation. The rule of the order can be summed up in one of its sentences: 'Let them remain alone in their own cells, or near them, meditating day and night on the law of the Lord, and watching in prayer, unless they are engaged in some other just occupations.' The Virgin was revered as the 'perfect Christian expression of the prophetic vocation,' and Marian devotion would remain a cornerstone of Carmelite life.

As with most programs that deny human frailty and desire, the Carmelites, transplanted to Europe, deviated from their lofty aims. By the time Saint Teresa of Ávila joined the order in 1535, the mystic found it ripe for the rigorous reforms she brought to bear, all of which sought to return the community to its original purpose of holding souls in uninterrupted communion with God. But Saint Teresa, for whom Thérèse Martin had been named, was the rare creature in whom sacrifice was greeted by joy and humor, an élan that her spiritual descendants were unable to preserve or replicate. The Lisieux Carmel was not high-spirited, nor, in contrast to a socially active *congréganiste* order, was it youthful, especially not in the eyes of a teenager: the average age was forty-seven. Among the twenty-six nuns remained one of the foundresses of the convent, Mother Geneviève, now eighty-three. Ill and silent, considered holy, she was waiting in the darkened choir for Thérèse; she 'fixed' her eyes on the newest member of the community, thrilling Thérèse, who embraced every moment of her entrance with joy.

Given a postulant's habit, a long blue dress with a black cape and bonnet, Thérèse was shown to her cell in order to change forever out of the clothes of a daughter of the French middle class. Pretty things that had once given cause for scruples, even a hat so piously pretty as the one she'd worn to Christmas mass with her father, navy blue trimmed with a decorative symbol of the Holy Spirit, a white dove, would trouble her no more. Her room on the second floor measured a little over six by twelve feet, a room to herself but one she was henceforth to refer to as 'our,' never 'my,' as she no longer had any property of her own. In her cell was a bed – a board laid on two trestles with a straw mattress, wool sheets, and pillow; a jug of water and basin set on the swept plank floor; a bench (not a chair); a writing desk and workbasket; and a few devotional books. While the nuns of Carmel kept silence, the walls around them spoke. 'My daughter, what are you doing here?' Thérèse's cell asked, lest she forget her calling.

True to the intentions of its original founder, life in the Lisieux Carmel sought to sanctify every minute and every action, to consecrate the entire being to God. The community rose at five, awakened by the snap of castanets in the hall, a reminder of the Spanish mystic's stringent reforms. Upon rising, the sisters dressed in their tunics, habits, toques, and veils; winter and summer they slipped their feet into the hemp sandals of Spanish peasants, *alpargatas*. Work and prayer came before food, hours before. A ten o'clock breakfast was preceded by a bell summoning the sisters to examine their consciences. In pairs they processed to the refectory, singing the De Profundis, taking their assigned places at the long tables, speaking only to confess a fault. They ate in silence and in unison, napkins stretched between their plates and their chests so as to catch, and consume, every crumb. A human skull hung on the wall above them, between lines of scripture, lest they forget, while they ate, the future of their bodies. Convent food was simple, two meals a day, with no meat, no eggs, milk, or butter during Lent or on Fridays. As the youngest – and the one most obviously willing if not anxious for mortification – Thérèse was given scraps that the others didn't want, 'food that had been left over or rejected at a previous meal' (reheated fish heads were an example furnished by Céline), 'food that even a healthy stomach would have had difficulty putting up with.'

The largest portion of the day was given to prayer in the choir, including mass, two hours of silent prayer, and three and a half hours of reciting the Divine Office. Also known as the Liturgy of the Hours – Matins, Prime, Terce, Sext, None, and Vespers – the Divine Office means literally 'a duty accomplished for God,' a daily cycle of devotions established in the sixth century with even more ancient, Judaic roots. (The Psalms and, later, the Acts of the Apostles include references to the recitation of prayers at particular hours.) For the Carmelites, there were also five hours of manual labor; two hours of recreation, during which edifying conversation was permitted; and one hour of free time before bed, which Thérèse used for writing. A naturally talkative person who had grown up depending on language to bridge all divides, even that between the dead and the living, she had chosen a life of separation and imposed silences, one that produced an outpouring of documents invaluable to her biographers: letters, poems, plays, memoirs, and notes, even scribbles, through which we can trace her spiritual evolution.

'I found the religious life to be exactly as I imagined it,' Thérèse recalled, which was not to say that there weren't trials. She knew nothing of sewing or sweeping or weeding. Every task she was given she completed slowly, only to be criticized for her clumsiness, her lack of accomplishment. And, most painful, she fell victim to an affection for Mother Marie de Gonzague that she herself understood as inappropriate, suffering an attraction so strong that she described it as if it were literal magnetism. Each day she invented 'a thousand reasons' to see the prioress; she had to 'walk rapidly by [her] door and to cling firmly to the banister of the staircase in order not to turn back.'

Later, as novice mistress in 1892, Thérèse would be able to see a familiar fault in the novice Martha of Jesus, an orphan whose neediness must have reminded her of herself during her postulancy. 'Your fondness for Mother Prioress is too natural,' she told the novice. 'She is doing your soul a great deal of harm, because you love her passionately, and those kinds of feelings displease God; in nuns they are poison. You did not become a Carmelite to satisfy your natural longings; you did so to mortify them and die to yourself.' It's interesting that Thérèse said that Mother Marie was doing Martha's soul a great deal of harm. It was a judgment she would never be able to apply to the prioress with regard to herself.

Of course, it is not possible to overstate Thérèse's vulnerability to any mother figure, to an available female outline onto which she could project her desire for a mother, and Marie de Gonzague was not anyone, but a woman of great charm. A daughter of the nobility, more brightly polished

and better educated than most in her position, she intended
to direct the affections of her twenty-five 'daughters.' More-
over, Thérèse's crush was not new, but had begun – was
deliberately cultivated – when she had suffered the diabolic illness that had culminated in a vision of the Virgin. In the
years following this manifestation of divine favor, Mother
Marie broke the Rule to allow Pauline to communicate with
Thérèse during Lent, she granted the sisters the indulgence of
long visits in the parlor, and she herself kissed and embraced
Thérèse in person and in messages appended to Pauline's
letters.

'Doesn't my angel want to come and be with her older sisters, who are so happy in God's service?' she asked when
Thérèse was ill in 1887.

'Tell dear mother that her Theresita loves her with all her
heart,' Thérèse answered.

By the time she entered, for six years Marie de Gonzague
had beckoned powerfully to Thérèse, one of the promises of
the cloister: a mother who found her adorable, compelling,
virtuous.

Whether or not it was wise to welcome a large faction of
blood sisters into the Carmel, the Martin daughters made
attractive postulants. Poised and well educated, they came
from material stability, which indicated a truer vocation than
those of nuns whose worldly position was low enough to
make the convent an agreeable alternative to a secular life of
drudgery and compromise. And they provided worthy
adversaries for the proud Marie de Gonzague; they were
more satisfying to order around.

'God permitted that she was very severe without her even being aware of it,' Thérèse wrote of the prioress, a generous interpretation of a woman every other nun remembered as mercurial, even irresponsible. During testimony, Marie of the Sacred Heart, Thérèse's oldest sister, was 'bound to say' that the community had a troubled atmosphere – 'deplorable disturbances: factions and personality clashes arising chiefly from the vexatious temperament of Mother Marie de Gonzague.' According to Céline, who would enter Carmel six years after Thérèse and whose remarks about the prioress were generally more compassionate than censorious, Mother Marie's many directives were 'based on the whim of the moment,' 'a legion of petty regulations,' in the words of another nun, 'which she repealed or changed according to her fancy,' made and forgotten so quickly that the other nuns ignored them.

But not Thérèse. She carried out every minute directive, blessed by the ability to see grace in every one of her superior's actions. If Mother Marie seemed to be cruel, it was with the purpose of advancing Thérèse's spiritual growth. Thérèse could not conclude what others saw plainly – that the prioress, whom one novice privately named 'the wolf,' required an environment of emotional turmoil in which 'precautions were necessary to avoid offending her susceptibilities.' In this female world, gestures were weapons: an averted face, a closed door, a smile withheld – any of these could wound.

Of course, Thérèse was not the humble downtrodden field flower she chose to portray, but a hothouse hybrid. She'd been orphaned, ill, coddled. Pauline and Marie lobbied constantly – humiliatingly, from Thérèse's perspective – for their little sister's being excused from one or another rigor of convent life. It was too cold, they insisted, for her to wear straw sandals, she must have fur-lined slippers, quickly provided by her aunt Guérin. And her bereft father came almost every day with fish, fruit, champagne, cakes, even a surprise so indulgent as 'an artificial melon which burst to scatter a rain of sweets.'

'Your little queen is crushed under the weight and the magnificence of your gifts,' Thérèse wrote in thanks and, it would seem, censure for the *Point d'Alençon* lace Louis delivered months too early for her clothing ceremony. A few years hence, farther along her path toward selflessness, she might have avoided so potentially hurtful a verb as *crushed* when thanking a frail father who would have no other wedding dresses to trim. But for now his doting compromised her before the community, who shared the treats heaped upon their newest member even as they faulted her for being a spoiled elitist.

As many have had the chance to observe, the cloister doesn't encourage charity as well as it does pettiness and jealousy. Thérèse would find that the most effective mortification came at the hands of her convent sisters. In Carmel, she would learn, as one of her novices testified, 'to transform all of her actions, even the least of them, into acts of love.' This meant responding with genuine sweet simplicity to a taunt; it meant sitting next to the most cross and disapproving sister at recreation; it meant looking everywhere for an opportunity to put another's happiness before her own.

There was an obvious formula, a simple Gospel directive she could apply to the impossible demands she made of herself. On one occasion when she was acting as assistant portress, she was asked to get up in the night and bring a lantern for Mother Marie's family, guests at the Carmel (in defiance of the Rule). To conquer herself and what she described as her violent thoughts against authority, Thérèse imagined that she was performing the chore for the Virgin and the Baby Jesus. 'And then I did it with incredible care, not leaving on it the least speck of dust.' She transformed the irritating demand into a joyful – thrilling – occasion to play a game that was over the heads of her sisters, a strategy she would have occasion to use again and again. After all, she intended to be not just a good religious but a saint.

DISORIENTED in the wake of his separation from Thérèse and troubled by Céline's announcement that she, too, planned to enter Carmel even as Léonie readied herself to reenter the Visitation, Louis Martin ran away from Lisieux on June 23, 1888. The next day, a telegram arrived at Les Buissonnets asking that money be sent to him in care of the post office at Le Havre but withholding his exact whereabouts. Sixty-five years old, Monsieur Martin was afflicted with dizziness and memory loss, with abrupt disturbances of mood. He had suffered a stroke; his kidneys were failing. Though he supported all his daughters' vocations, he was happiest in his role as father and must have been oppressed by the idea of an imminent and lonely death.

Céline, accompanied by her uncle Isidore Guérin and her cousin Ernest Maudelonde, went to Le Havre to watch for her father at the entrance to the post office, where, on the 27th, she found him and escorted him home.

Four months later, distraught at the departure of his confessor and spiritual director, Père Pichon, Louis Martin broke down again. His mental state remained precarious enough that Thérèse's clothing ceremony – her reception of the habit – and thus the beginning of her novitiate were delayed. Most postulants wait six months; Thérèse waited nine.

The ceremony, on January 10, 1889, went more smoothly than the family could have hoped. Monsieur Martin was able to attend, to see his daughter dressed as a bride, trimmed in Alençon lace, and to witness her laughing delight in an unexpected fall of snow. Just as rain in Rome had arrived to drown impatient hopes, here was another, happier celestial message. 'What thoughtfulness on the part of Jesus!' she exclaimed of the 'little miracle,' devoting paragraphs of her notebooks to this 'incomprehensible condescension' from Jesus, in a voice at once girlishly naive and infuriatingly self-important. Thérèse does give her readers ample occasion to note the inescapable – the divisive and yet potentially transcendent – subjectivity of human experience. 'The monastery garden was white like me!' Thérèse marveled. She received the snow as a gift from her Bridegroom, and so for her it was.

Two days before, she had written to her father from her retreat, telling her 'incomparable king' of the crown of tribulations Jesus was preparing him, one that was not yet, alas not nearly, complete. The following month, Louis Martin succumbed to hallucinations so violent that Isidore Guérin judged him dangerous to those around him, to his daughters Céline and Léonie, and to the maid, Maria Cosseron. 'He was seeing frightful things,' Céline explained in a letter to a family friend, 'slaughter, battles; he was hearing the sounds of cannon and the drum.' The soldier's son no longer knew where, or who, he was. What's more, he was carrying a loaded revolver. With the help of a friend, Isidore Guérin disarmed Monsieur Martin and, on February 12, 1889, escorted him to the Bon Sauveur mental asylum in Caen.

'Jesus is a spouse of blood,' Thérèse wrote back to Céline. 'Our dear father must be much loved by Jesus to have to suffer this way.'

At every opportunity, the Martin daughters reassured one another of the spiritual benefits to be reaped by their father's disgrace, even as they were shamed by a public breakdown that local gossip attributed to the strain of Thérèse's vocation. Their interpretation of their father's mental disintegration was not as self-serving as it might seem; at least, it was not theirs alone. In his moments of clarity, Monsieur Martin himself embraced his trial. A letter from Céline to Pauline, Marie, and Thérèse reported that Louis had told his doctor he had never had any humiliations in his life and he 'needed one.'

The removal of her father to a distant asylum – no more visits, no more gifts – and of Céline, who went to Caen to be near him, pushed Thérèse farther along her lonely path, so that she might practice 'putting my self-love in its proper place, i.e., under my feet.' She worked in the refectory, an assignment that gave her ample invitations to overcome selfishness. Charged with preparing the bread in an alcove infested with spiders, she had to steel herself against those creatures that had always frightened and disgusted her, and she had to work silently in the company of Pauline, with whom she longed to speak.

'Taken up, at this time, with a real attraction for objects

that were both very ugly and the least convenient,' Thérèse explored a predilection that would only grow. Given humble tools with which to work, she found them insufficiently inconvenient and traded them for the nearly useless objects she found abandoned in the attic, among them a lamp whose wick would not turn, requiring that she raise and lower it by means of a pin. When her petite and pretty water jug was replaced with a big ugly one, 'all chipped,' she embraced it with joy. Thérèse's pleasure in the ugly and the rejected, in learning to manipulate a new aesthetic, recalls the fetishism of her childhood altars to the Virgin/Zélie, to Pauline. Never detached from material objects, never indifferent, Thérèse had traded bibelots for punishments, each promising a minute but significant spiritual advancement.

Determined to become a genius of secret mortification, she discovered opportunity everywhere; if she sat, she would not lean against her backrest. Mistakenly accused of breaking a vase, she seized the chance to prostrate herself and kiss the floor, grateful for the injustice. Years ago, in her first life, she had refused her mother's offer of a sou for such abasement and called her refusal a sin of pride. Now she was hungry for occasions to redress that mistake. Without Zélie to receive the penance herself, it was a gesture that bore endless repetition.

And yet, what was Thérèse's insistence on being last if not the means of making herself first: a new and subtler manifestation of pride? Was her determination to suffer all insults and privations in silence one she (unconsciously) imagined would be vindicated by the eventual publication of her written account?

In her letters from this period of her novitiate, Thérèse returned over and over to the theme of littleness, referring to herself as a grain of sand, an image she borrowed from Pauline, who, in the week preceding Thérèse's entry into Carmel, had spoken of advantages given the small: 'Always littler, lighter, in order to be lifted more easily by the breeze of love.' This symbol of the most hidden and fleet of souls (originally from the prayer of General de Sonis, quoted in Père Pichon's October 1887 retreat sermon) possessed Thérèse, and the remainder of her life would be defined by retreat and subtraction. She who had abandoned the world outside the cloister walls found the microcosm of the community within too large.

Consumed by her struggle not merely to achieve mastery over self but to reduce that self, to strip away need and preference – desires as seemingly innocent and humble as those for a warm bed, a tablemate who didn't insult or rebuke her – Thérèse consecrated her every sacrifice to God, for the purpose of saving souls. But the habit of self-abnegation promised a mortal salvation, too, one that would have been deeply compelling to Thérèse, who never admitted so heretical an agenda, or even consciously acknowledged it. Absolute impoverishment confers absolute power. What – who – could be taken away from her?

In the monastery garden, in a grotto honoring Mary Magdalene, Thérèse received what she described as a mystical grace, an experience that underscored the attractions of hiddenness: 'It was as though a veil had been cast over all the things of this earth for me,' she later told her sister Pauline. 'I was entirely hidden under the Blessed Virgin's veil. . . . I recall doing things as though not doing them; it was as if someone lent me a body.' The feeling persisted for a week, granting her unusual peace of mind.

More often, she was tormented by loneliness, sometimes literally knocking and calling for an elusive God. In 1911, Martha of Jesus, who had been a novice under the spiritual guidance of Thérèse, gave testimony during the beatification process that her mistress stood at the door of the tabernacle, saying, 'Are you there, Jesus? Answer me, I beg you.'

God was silent, and He was slow. As with her entrance and her clothing ceremony, Thérèse's taking her vows was delayed; because of her youth she would spend eight months longer than the standard year as an unprofessed novice. As 1889 ended, her old home in the world, Les Buissonnets, was dismantled, the furniture divided among the Guérins and the Carmel, a promotion for Monsieur Martin's clock, now marking the hours of the Divine Office in the choir. In the world outside the cloister, Céline, twenty, was suffering heart trouble brought on by strain: the illness of their father and the chronic conflict within her. Having declared she would enter Carmel, she couldn't quite imagine being imprisoned in a cloister. Or perhaps she imagined it too well: she couldn't yet turn her back on the world and all it offered.

Months earlier, Céline had written Thérèse an account of a dream she'd had. Dreams were not a usual subject of the sisters' correspondence, but this was not an ordinary dream. In it, Thérèse was dragged into the woods and killed by an anonymous man. The martyrdom of her younger sister quickly and unambiguously accomplished, heralded by birds singing and smoke rising (the Vatican's signal to the world of a new pope), Céline was grieved to find herself left behind, 'wandering in the countryside,' when, as she recounted, 'a little boy, a shoemaker's apprentice, jumped on me and plunged his awl several times into my throat. I was so happy that I had no thought of running away, but the child being undoubtedly too weak, I did not die. However his rage increased more and more, and he ended up by tearing out my eyes. This time I collapsed but saying always: more more!'

As with Pauline's fantasy of the Christ Child fondling and rending his ball, Céline's images are startling for their violence, their nearly undisguised sexuality, but Thérèse did not respond to those aspects. Instead she shot back the peculiar observation that 'Céline's dream is very pretty,' along with the platitudinous, knee-jerk advice that we 'let Jesus tear from us all that is most dear.' Could she have read the letter without some attempt to understand Céline's agony? As always, Thérèse urged her sister toward self-privation; she ignored what she was perhaps unable as well as unwilling to acknowledge, the unappeased passion of Céline's more usually hidden psyche.

'I attach no importance to dreams,' Thérèse would write when she was twenty-three, dismissing the lush Eden of her imagination, dreams of forests and beaches, of laughing children and animals, because, as she judged, 'they are never mystical.' She plumbed them for religious messages and found none, not even in 'birds the like of which [she'd] never seen before,' a seemingly obtuse comment from one who every day had occasion to note the Holy Spirit as a dove, and who described herself, her spiritual flights and falls, in terms of a robin, a magpie, a swallow, a duck, an owl, an ostrich, a bluebird, a chick, a sparrow. Familiar birds provided waking metaphors, but the caution that prevented her from allowing Céline's dreams their significance also refused the fantastic creatures that soared through her own sleep.

Perhaps her education, largely via Pauline, had taught Thérèse to distrust fantasy as well as other forms of liberation. The images she used consciously were not those she invented but those she received.

At the end of July 1890, Canon Delatroëtte wrote Thérèse that, while he still considered her 'too young to take on irrevocable promises,' he would no longer forbid her asking Bishop Hugonin's consent to make her profession of vows. The bishop granted his permission and two dates were set: September 8 for the intimate, cloistered ceremony, and September 24 for her public reception of the black veil. On September 2, Thérèse received Pope Leo's apostolic benediction, which included his blessing on her 'saintly and venerable father, tried by suffering.'

Her cousin Jeanne Guérin, engaged to Doctor la Neele (the same who would attend Thérèse at the end of her life), visited the Carmel and showed Thérèse an invitation to the October 1 wedding, which the newly professed nun would be unable to attend. As suggestible and eager for romance as any other girl her age, Thérèse used it as a guide to create an invitation (never sent) for the event she awaited:

Almighty God, Creator of Heaven and earth, Sovereign Ruler of the World, and the most glorious Virgin Mary, Queen and Princess of the heavenly Court, wish to invite you to the wedding of their Divine Son Jesus, King of Kings and Lord of Lords, to Mademoiselle Thérèse Martin, now Lady and Princess of the kingdoms bought as dowry by her Divine Spouse, namely the Childhood of Jesus and His Passion, her titles of nobility being: of the Child Jesus and of the Holy Face.

Monsieur Louis Martin, Proprietor and Owner of the Domains of Suffering and Humiliation, and Madame Martin, Princess and Lady of Honor of the Heavenly Court, wish to invite you to the wedding of their Daughter Thérèse to Jesus, the Word of God, Second Person of the Adorable Trinity, who, through the Operation of the Holy Spirit, was made Man and Son of Mary, the Queen of Heaven.

Unable to invite you to the nuptial blessing given on the mountain of Carmel (the heavenly court alone was admitted) they beg you, nonetheless, to be present at the return from the Wedding which will take place tomorrow, on the day of Eternity, to which Day Jesus, the Son of God, will come on the clouds of Heaven to judge the Living and the Dead.

The hour is uncertain as yet, so you are invited to hold yourselves in readiness and to watch.

Writing in loneliness, promising herself to an invisible and withholding lover, giving voice to her dead mother, her father in a mental asylum, imagining guests too sublime to name, Thérèse could not have predicted the effect of this schoolgirl exercise – an effort that might be parody, were it not so palpably earnest – on her modern readers, abruptly transformed into voyeurs. Surely, we weren't meant to witness such nakedness; surely, had Thérèse lived longer, she would have understood the invitation as juvenilia, utterly lacking the dignity she meant to convey. She may have been intellectually precocious, but, like most seventeen-year-olds, Thérèse had yet to acquire restraint, let alone style. She shared the 'amusement' with her sisters, who had taught her the language of religious romance, and she sent it to Père Pichon in Canada; later, she used it to teach her novices how glorious were the titles of a bride of Christ when compared to the material riches offered by an earthly union. At the time, the lesson was one she still struggled to accept, at least emotionally.

A retreat in anticipation of her 'irrevocable promises' was characterized by the 'absolute aridity' that would come to define her life as a nun. Dry, denied any hint of God's presence, waiting for consolation that never arrived, waiting without encouragement, she found a mirror for her anguish in Saint John of the Cross, whose mystical writings would inspire her ultimate spiritual ambition:

> To enjoy the taste of all things, have no taste for anything.
> To know all things, learn to know nothing.
> To possess all things, resolve to possess nothing.
> To be all things, be willing to be nothing.

This exalted nothingness, however, was found on the other side of doubt, abandonment, destitution. On the eve of her profession, while making the stations of the cross, Thérèse succumbed to panic. What she wanted was beyond her. Her vocation was a sham. She went to Marie of the Angels for help, half hoping the novice mistress would agree with her and dismiss her from the Carmel, but Marie of the Angels received Thérèse's confession as a cleansing act of humility, a reassurance of limited use against what Thérèse would come to regard as a visitation from the devil. Perhaps the prioress could help? Summoned from the choir, mother Marie de Gonzague 'simply laughed' at her fears.

The next day, prostrated on the ground in front of the community, she was 'flooded with a river of peace.' As was the custom, against her heart she wore her letter of profession, which she had written during her retreat.

Oh Jesus, my Divine Spouse! May I never lose the second robe of my baptism! Take me before I can commit the slightest voluntary fault. May I never seek nor find anything but Yourself alone. May creatures be nothing for me, and may I be nothing for them, but may You, Jesus, be *everything!* May the things of earth never be able to trouble my soul, and may nothing disturb my peace. Jesus, I ask You for nothing but peace, and also love, infinite love without any limits other than Yourself; love which is no longer I but You, my Jesus. Jesus, may I die a martyr for You. Give me martyrdom of heart or of body, or rather give me both. Give me the grace to fulfill my Vows in all their perfection, and make me understand what a real spouse of Yours should be. Never let me be a burden to the community, let nobody be occupied with me, let me be looked upon as one to be trampled underfoot, forgotten like Your little grain of sand, Jesus. May Your will be done in me perfectly, and may I arrive at the place You have prepared for me.

Jesus, allow me to save very many souls; let no soul be lost today; let all the souls in purgatory be saved. Jesus, pardon me if I say anything I should not say. I want only to give You joy and to console You.

Written without imagining the distractions of a guest list, an audience, Thérèse's letter of profession strikes a much clearer note of sincerity than does the invitation. Never intended for anyone else's eyes, it convinces.

On September 24, during the public ceremony, Thérèse found herself young enough, alone enough, to weep over the absence of Bishop Hugonin, ill in Bayeux; Père Pichon, in Canada; and her own father, still confined in the asylum. Pauline chastised her for being so unrealistic as to expect their father's presence, or even to want it, knowing what risks it would present. Thérèse knew she was weak, needy, a person of 'little resources' who found this important day filled with 'sadness and bitterness.' Wearing a crown and carrying a crucifix Céline had taken to Caen so that Monsieur Martin might touch and bless them, she took small consolation from these surrogates, which may have provided her father his own portion of agony.

Still, she was determined in her vocation, and what was pain if not a step toward martyrdom? No one judged her as harshly as she did herself.

Writing of the occasion to the prioress of the Tours

Carmel, Mother Marie de Gonzague said of Thérèse: 'The angelic child is seventeen and a half, and she has the judgment of one of thirty, the religious perfection of an old perfected novice, and possession of herself; she is a perfect religious.'

January of 1891 brought unusually low temperatures. Only the refectory was heated; the nuns' cells were frigid, their bedding inadequate. Later, Thérèse would remember that she thought she would die of the cold. But she made no complaint; she was relieved to be launched on her career as a professed nun, spared the humiliations of fur-lined slippers and rules relaxed for her presumed weakness.

As was more and more clear, the repetitious quality of cloistered life trapped the sisters in time as well as place. Much as the Divine Office was intended to provide an environment of spiritual exaltation, relentless striving toward the holy often induced its opposite: exhaustion, lack of feeling, the emotional depletion from which many religious suffer. The memory of her brief ecstasy, along with the gilded histories of spiritual ancestors such as Teresa of Ávila and Magdalen de' Pazzi, Carmelites who sustained raptures for hours on end, who reported the embarrassment of uncontrollable levitation, must have tortured poor Thérèse, with her taste for dramatic manifestations, her orphan's ravenous need for reassurance. She read John of the Cross, she revered his ability to lose himself in Christ, and yet she held herself in check. How could a girl who prayed to be taken before she had a chance to sin overcome her suspicion of abandoned experience?

The annual October retreat, her first as a professed nun, was led by a Franciscan, Father Prou, who spoke expansively on the themes of abandonment and mercy. Prou, a last-minute replacement who specialized in big, excitable crowds, offered the more inhibited Carmelites a respite from their usual fare of sin and punishment. The community as a whole didn't like this, but Thérèse, whose soul was a 'book in which this priest read better than I did myself,' found him to be a generous and profoundly influential confessor. Whatever faults Thérèse had, he assured her, they caused God no offense. He told her that she was, in fact, good, and the praise was a catalyst.

'My nature was such that fear made me recoil; with love not only did I advance, I actually flew.' Unexpectedly released from anxiety, Thérèse was launched toward her ultimate vision of herself as a drop lost in an ocean of divine acceptance. This evolution within Thérèse, as yet incomplete, from a concern with judgment toward a doctrine of love, reflected a nineteenth-century trend within French Catholicism, one for which the young nun's life and work would provide its most intense expression.

In December of 1891, Mother Geneviève died. Thérèse witnessed the moment of the saintly old nun's 'birth in heaven,' the first time she had assisted at such a 'ravishing' spectacle since the death of her own mother. She spent two hours at the foot of the bed, later admitting a 'sort of insensibility,' but sure, when death was finally accomplished, of a 'joy and fervor,' a little vicarious jolt of the ecstasy of arriving in heaven. Eager for relics, she saw a tear glistening from one of the old woman's eyelashes and crept back in the evening, 'unseen by anyone,' to harvest it with a bit of linen. She kept the tear against her heart, in the pocket where she kept her vows.

A few days later, she who insisted on the meaninglessness of her disappointing and 'never mystical' dreams went to bed and dreamed the revered foundress was making her will, bequeathing something of value to each of the nuns of Carmel. When Thérèse's turn arrived after all the others', she feared that there was nothing left, that all had been given away. But Mother Geneviève turned to her. '"To you I leave my heart",' she said, and 'she repeated this three times with great emphasis.' As told by Thérèse, the dream resonates with the tones of a parable: slow and symbol-laden, like a processional marking a feast day. At the time, Thérèse accepted it as consolation. Later, while writing her *Story of a Soul*, it would seem a prophecy.

Less than a week after Mother Geneviève was buried, the convent was struck by influenza. All but three nuns, one of whom was Thérèse, were too ill to get up. 'My nineteenth birthday was celebrated with a death,' she remembered of January 2, 1892, her words without irony. After Sister Saint Joseph came Sister Magdalene, of whose release Thérèse had had a presentiment; and then the subprioress, Sister Fébronie, died. Thérèse cared for the sick and assumed duties others had been forced to lay aside. She who shrank from a spider 'did not have the least bit of fear' of death but found herself excited, in part by its passport 'to a better life,' even more by the chance to show that she could handle real responsibility. Thérèse was no longer the spoiled little sister who had arrived not knowing how to sweep the stairs. In the wake of the crisis, she was much praised, even by her old foe Canon Delatroëtte.

A different triumph followed. The attenuated conflict over Céline's vocation was resolved. The last of the Martins to choose the life of a religious, Céline had struggled for years with issues of 'purity' – sexual attraction – and with a genuine interest in the world outside the cloister. She'd been courted, and men had proposed to her; she was tempted by a life very different from that chosen by her sisters. Looking back as a forty-year-old on her late teens and early twenties, Céline would remember the period as one of danger, her vocation 'so close to foundering . . . holding on only by a thread.' At nineteen, outside a convent, without the support of a community of like-minded souls, she had taken a vow of chastity and struggled to keep it, receiving letter after letter from Thérèse, who described the soul's relationship to God in terms of flowers with treasures 'known only by bees,' flowers blooming in readiness for Jesus to pluck, while in the meantime the angel bees 'draw out all the honey' – a fervent tangle of sentiment and suggestion, all of which was meant to convince Céline to rebuff earthly suitors and wait for Christ, her incomparable and holy gardener.

For years, Henri Maudelonde, a nephew of the Guérins, had pursued Céline aggressively. An attorney in Caen, he came frequently to see her at the home of her aunt and uncle, where he was always seated next to Céline, a position he won because he protested furiously at any other arrangement. After dinner, he would take her in his arms and dance, holding her to himself.

Having experienced the fleeting excitement of a flirtation in Italy, knowing the pleasure of pretty clothes and compliments from admirers, Thérèse was very alert to the temptation of earthly romance. Without the protection of Christ, she said, she 'could have fallen as low as St. Mary Magdalene,' a judgment more in the realm of melodrama than of possibility. She always gave God credit for her remarkable, if desperate, self-control – and she was sufficiently troubled by the idea of free will to consistently pray that any freedom to offend God be taken from her. Unable to take responsibility for her own refusal of mortal attachment, Thérèse didn't have the emotional margin to express sympathy for her sister's profound conflict. Céline had allowed herself to consider another life, and while Thérèse never entertained such visions, the emotional strain of her sister's struggle was enough to provoke 'a torrent of tears,' as well as a relentless campaign of rhetoric and metaphor. She and Céline were twin souls, they were two flowers on the same stem. How could Céline 'tarnish' herself for a mere man, someone blind to 'the seal which the Spouse placed on [her] forehead,' proclaiming her the property of another, irresistible fiancé, Jesus? She would not have any sister of hers be like 'so many souls seduced by this false light, fly like poor moths and burn their wings.' Céline could not drink the 'poisoned cup of a too ardent love of creatures.'

Ready to project a vision of Christ onto every unattractive human canvas – the short-tempered nun, the hypocritical moralizer, the dishonest, the greedy, even the murderously evil – Thérèse refused, with perhaps greater determination, to admit the terrifying possibility of a mortal vessel for divine love. Human affection was a sham, a trick, a distraction, a means toward a fall. After all, her own devoted mother had abandoned her.

Despite misgivings and disappointment profound enough to undermine her health, Céline did rebuff Henri, and the attentive 'military type,' as Céline described him, courted another woman, Marie Asseline, who accepted his proposal of marriage. The wedding was set for April 20, 1892, a celebration Céline would be forced to attend, out of politeness. She remained, in her sister's quaint and awkward language, 'virginized,' but a last crisis presented itself in the form of the reception dance, to the idea of which Thérèse responded as if Céline had agreed to participate in an orgy, rather than what was for her sister more akin to a funeral, a good-bye to the other vocation she found 'beautiful': marriage.

To be fair, Thérèse's equation between dancing and sex was not her own. Traditional group dances like the gavotte (which resembles the minuet) and the quadrille had been increasingly eclipsed by the waltz and the polka; this was part of the contagion that had been brought by the invading Prussian army. The clergy was obsessed with the moral dangers of these new dances in which 'man and woman held each other closely and exclusively.' In some regions, priests went so far as to deny communion to those fallen girls who were known to have waltzed. Could Thérèse have been aware of the intimacies between Céline and Henri that had already taken place at the Guérins'? Determined to save her sister from peril, Thérèse let loose such a deluge of prayers and tears from behind the grille that when Céline at last attended the wedding, 'her partner found out he was totally powerless to make her dance.' To his great confusion, 'he was condemned simply to walking in order to conduct her to her place.' Thérèse's report has a distinctly fairy-tale ring, as if she'd managed to bewitch her sister's feet with her petitions.

Céline was so confused, so browbeaten, that she said she had 'lost the power to distinguish between the beautiful and the ugly.' She was going through 'a succession of voids . . . in darkness, reduced to the state of the log . . . in the most total incapacity.' If the image of the apprentice plunging his awl into her throat indicated a repressed and frustrated sexuality, the log was one of exhausted, paralytic depression. Two years remained before Céline would enter Carmel, years of continuing doubts and conflicts.

On May 10, 1892, Louis Martin left the Bon Sauveur mental asylum under the care of his brother-in-law Isidore Guérin. According to Madame Guérin, his morale was as good as it could be under the circumstances, but his limbs were too weak to support him. In his wheelchair, he 'cried all the time,' so overwhelmed was he by relief to be among family, reunited with two of his daughters, Céline and Léonie, under the Guérins' roof. He depended on a manservant to feed him, and when it was necessary to move him from chair to bed, 'he put his arms around the servant's neck, who then carried him.'

In his docility, his inclination to weep, Louis Martin was

like a child, and yet Céline knew that 'he understood and felt what children do not understand and feel.' On May 12, the Guérins took him to Carmel to visit Pauline, Marie, and Thérèse, who tried not to cry at so diminished a father. His speech was limited, but when they said, 'Au revoir,' see you again, he pointed upward and replied, 'Au ciel,' in heaven.

It would be their last visit with him, the only one in four years.

'YOU WANT TO CLIMB a mountain, and God wills to have you descend.'

During Thérèse's retreat in October of 1892, she tried to come to terms with the unavoidable paradox of Christianity. What way existed toward the sublime except through total loss and poverty? If asked where she lived, mustn't she be able to answer with Christ: 'The foxes have their lairs, the birds of heaven their nests, but I have no place to rest my head'?

'A question here of the interior,' she qualified in a letter she wrote to Céline just after the retreat, lest her sister think she meant anything as simple – as superficial – as renouncing food or shelter. Others might find her good, even exemplary, but mortal measures were worthless to Thérèse. She knew her virtues, even her love, to be flawed: flawed by self, a mirror too clouded to reflect the divine. Having begun to see her 'little way' toward union with Christ, she was eager to apply her intelligence, her will, and above all her faith to the discovery of any means to further her progress.

In order to more efficiently strip herself of self, she returned to the teachings in *The Imitation of Christ,* a work she knew well enough to recite. Desire to be unknown and counted as nothing, Thomas à Kempis advised. By now her application of the monk's formulae was almost reflexive. Mystical experience defied articulation, but Saint John of the Cross provided witness to the anguish of the soul's 'dark night,' the abyss into which she would have to fall before landing in the arms of God. She read and reread the Gospels, she turned to Christ in wordless prayer, attempting to open her heart to the possibility of grace. In her quest for union with God, she raked through her consciousness to find and expunge whatever might interfere with its absorption by the divine.

In February of 1893, Thérèse wrote the first of her fifty-four poems, most of them unremarkable as art, but useful for what insight they provide into her spiritual development. 'The Divine Dew, or The Virginal Milk of Mary,' was not a spontaneous outpouring – few of her works were – but a response to a request by Sister Teresa of Saint Augustine for a canticle (verses to be sung aloud) on the infancy of Jesus. The poem relies on a passage taken from Saint Augustine, who explains Mary as a conduit for the Word of God, a spiritual wet nurse whose breast transforms the adult nourishment of scripture into the milk of love. This somewhat patronizing exegesis, taken up by Saint Francis de Sales in his 'Treatise on the Love of God,' is made more distasteful by Thérèse's conflating milk with dew's 'abundant sap,' Jesus with a 'new bud, gracious and scarlet red,' a phallic flower who, crucified, bleeds milk. Such equations, or perhaps the eagerness to make such equations, result in a curiously uncomfortable aesthetic; still, they provide access to Thérèse's particular vision. Even as she discarded more and more of what might interfere with her spiritual ambition, those ideas and images she kept were subject to a process of rendering. She boiled them down until what she found in the eye of God was not infinite diversity but simplicity, identification, oneness.

On February 20, 1893, Pauline was elected prioress of Carmel and became Mother Agnes. As a novice rather than a chapter nun, Thérèse was spared the obligation of participating in the close and emotionally fraught election between the sister she revered and Marie de Gonzague. Pauline, young and intimidated by an older opponent who frankly intended to intimidate, had landed in a position that would test her diplomacy as well as her ingenuity. In a concession to Mother Marie de Gonzague's need to continue in her role as a spiritual director, and manipulator, Pauline appointed the former prioress novice mistress and made Thérèse her assistant. The work of guiding the novices would fall mostly to Thérèse, younger than the women she instructed and counseled, shy and awkward in her own estimation, without any talent for friendship.

The task was beyond her, and so, as she said, 'I threw myself into the arms of the Lord,' a vantage she compared to a castle turret, from which nothing could escape her divinely aided scrutiny, which she applied to each young woman in her individuality, seeing both strengths and weaknesses. Observant and uncompromising, Thérèse allied herself with her novices against their flaws, characterizing her methods as those of a little gundog, 'the one chasing game all day long. You realize the hunters (mistresses of novices and Prioresses) are too big to slip into the bushes, but a little dog . . . it has a sensitive nose and it slips in everywhere!' she wrote to Céline.

She was dogged, but not unimaginative. Over the next few years she would discover a talent for clarifying doctrine to those who had not received as much education as she. A kaleidoscope, whose three mirrors transform scraps of colored paper into beautiful designs, provided an inspired illustration for the Holy Trinity. When God considers His creation, He looks through His triune Self, ennobling it with His exalted vision. To retreat from God's eye would be to find ourselves reduced to scraps: worthless. Another cherished image was that of the newly invented elevator, a vehicle Thérèse used many times over to describe God's grace, a force that lifts us to heights we can't reach on our own.

Martha of Jesus, a novice who had spent her childhood in a series of orphanages and who was described by all as emotionally unbalanced, with a violent temper, gave witness to the unusual dedication and presence of her young teacher. Probably no one had shown her the patience and the love she received from Thérèse. 'Everything about her commanded respect,' Martha testified during the beatification process, noting that Thérèse deliberately 'sought out the company of those nuns whose temperaments she found hardest to bear' – part of the apprentice saint's self-imposed program of perfecting her sisterly love. What merit was there in acting charitably toward people whom one loved naturally? Thérèse went out of her way to spend time with, and therefore to love, the people she found repellent. It was an effective means of achieving interior poverty, a way to remove a place to rest her head.

In 1895, when Céline became one of Thérèse's novices, she observed her little sister's spiritual evolution. 'Oh when I think how much I have to acquire!' she said, despairing.

'Rather, how much you have to lose,' Thérèse answered.

For now, Céline was still in the world. In June of 1893, she moved their father to La Musse, the Guérins' summer home. He would be away from his daughters in Lisieux, but the countryside suited his temperament. Even if he couldn't fish, he would be calmed by trees, fields, water. Unaccompanied by Léonie, who had departed for the Visitation at Caen (this time for a two-year stay), Céline admitted a spasm of self-pity, 'considering [her]self with heartbreaking dizziness as the last stray of the family.' At La Musse, she devoted herself utterly to her father, to providing psychic insulation between the old man and his fears. A good-night kiss and a sign of the cross seemed to protect him from nightmares. 'It is as though I had become his mother,' she wrote with no small satisfaction to her three sisters in Carmel. But Céline was drained by her sacrifice and by the yet unresolved conflict over her vocation. Behind her words was an implicit grief: her role as nurse to a father infantilized by illness – and later to Thérèse, similarly diminished – would be as close as she would come to motherhood. Where was fulfillment?

'Within me there is always nothing, always the dark night,' she wrote.

In September of 1893, Thérèse, having been a professed novice for the standard three years, asked not to be promoted but to continue as a novice indefinitely. On the face of it, the request seems odd for a nun so impatient for spiritual advancement, and yet it represented her ambition. She who would be first guarded her position at last, permanently subservient within the community. As a novice she would always have to ask permission of the other, full sisters: she would never be elected to any position of importance. Within a closed hierarchy, fraught with lobbying and shifting alliances, she found an obvious way to follow Thomas à Kempis's advice to be submissive to everyone, to protect herself from the dangers of pride. Remaining closely associated with the other novices, she could continue to care for her spiritual charges, especially Martha of Jesus, who had yet another year as a novice and who was troubled – needy – in ways Thérèse felt she could address.

Having chosen to stay a perpetual child within the religious community, still, twenty-one years old in 1894, Thérèse could assume one privilege of her majority: she was now allowed to fast during Lent. And, in a shift that impresses itself upon biographers combing through the most tangible and personal of her effects – her writing – she abandoned the 'proper' slanting penmanship Pauline had insisted she use as a student and began to write the faster, vertical script that came naturally to her. Clean and consistent and highly legible, without decorative or indulgent elements, it has only one distinctive flourish: the backward loop of the lowercase *d*.

The year 1894 brought a national celebration of Joan of Arc, whose beatification was at last authorized on January 27. Thérèse wrote two plays in honor of her childhood heroine, the first about Joan's response to the heavenly voices calling her to battle, the second about her resulting martyrdom. The plays were to be performed during the community's recreations, and Thérèse invested a great deal of time and attention, a great deal of herself, in their creation. Joan's acceptance of her mission echoes Thérèse's Christmas conversion – a transformative grace – and the Maid of Orléans voices a Carmelite's preference for a life of hidden poverty rather than glory. At the time of her writing, Thérèse was considering requesting a transfer to a place where she'd be truly hidden, the Carmel of Saigon, a separation from her family that would offer both spiritual rewards and terrors. Aside from the romance she had always seen in foreign missions, a geographic remove might grant her emotional independence from the sisters whom she loved and who persisted in babying her.

Afraid of what was to come, Thérèse's Joan of Arc girds herself for battles she never imagined fighting. Thérèse, whose chronic sore throats and hoarseness were now accompanied by pains in her chest, would also have to prepare herself for a martyrdom different from those of her fantasies. Her blood would be spilled, but as she would reflect on her deathbed, an infirmary was not the arena she'd once pictured: it wasn't the Colosseum with its soldiers and its lions but an internal and seemingly interminable struggle, hidden from all: minute. Still, as she wrote to Léonie in Caen, 'Everything is so big in religion . . . to pick up a pin out of love can convert a soul.'

On Sunday, May 27, 1894, Louis Martin had a stroke and was administered the last sacraments at the Guérins' house in La

Musse. On June 5, he had a heart attack, serious enough, Céline reported, that he 'turned blue and his heart was no longer beating.' Isidore Guérin revived him with ether, and the family settled in to a deathwatch, marked by the hysteria familiar to such situations. Céline, Marie Guérin, Doctor and Jeanne la Neele, together with a seminarian friend, Abbé Cornière, distracted themselves with a photographic project, 'a story of travelers in living pictures,' posed at various sites around the country house where Louis lay dying. 'We spend our days in uncontrollable laughter, enough to split our sides, and I am thirsting for solitude. I can no longer breathe. Then I am unhappy,' Céline wrote Thérèse.

For Céline, the grief of their father's imminent death was complicated by the increasing pressure of invitations from Père Pichon to join him in Canada, where, as early as 1891, he had urged her to become the foundress of his Bethany Institute, which sought to provide a moral education for neglected children. Probably it seemed to him a perfect solution to Céline's predicament of a religious impulse coupled with a desire to remain in the world. And it must also have seemed something her family would oppose. At his request, she kept the plan secret, acknowledging her vocational conflict in veiled terms of sacrifice, journeys, separations required by God, vague allusions that flummoxed and disturbed her Carmelite sisters. Privately, miserably, Céline struggled with the idea of leaving versus that of joining an order in which she would be reunited with three of her siblings, a prospect that might present itself falsely as a vocation.

On July 29, Louis Martin at last died, with Céline beside him. All the daughters welcomed their father's release from illness; they celebrated his having accomplished what they believed was a living purgatory. Directly, he would be on his way to God, to Zélie, to the four children he'd lost so many years before. 'In a sleep filled with anguish, I suddenly awakened,' Céline wrote of the night following his death. 'I saw in the firmament a kind of luminous globe. . . . And this globe went deeply into the immensity of heaven.'

Freed at last from the care of her father, Céline turned to the question of Canada; she revealed Père Pichon's invitation to her sisters. Thérèse immediately launched a campaign to win a fourth Martin sister's entry to the Carmel. She might flirt with the idea of hiding herself in Indochina, but it was impossible that her soul mate, the other of the 'two drops of dew' that would soon 'be united for eternity in the bosom of the divine Sun' should pursue her mortal destiny on the other side of the Atlantic. Thérèse succumbed to an emotional storm that echoed her panic over her abandonment by Pauline and Marie and that was perhaps exacerbated by her already failing health. She cried herself into severe headaches and sought a cure in a typically economical program of two-for-one petitionary prayer: she wanted a sign from God that her father was with Him, a sign other than a luminous orb. If the obdurate Sister Aimée of Jesus (the mouthpiece of the community's misgivings) relented in her reasonable opposition to another Martin's joining the order – an artist, no less, rather than a person of more useful talents – then Thérèse would know that 'Papa went *straight to heaven.*'

Improbably, Sister Aimée changed her mind, Mother Gonzague acquiesced, Mother Agnes approved, Père Pichon withdrew, Canon Delatroëtte made no objection. Often, it must have seemed that the sole way to explain the collapse of so many potential obstacles to the agenda of Sister Thérèse was that her will was aligned with God's. The only person who seemed unhappy with the turn of events was Céline. 'Once I made the resolution to enter Carmel as early as possible, disgust invaded my soul, repugnance for the religious life.' But Thérèse read her sister's resistance as an auspicious sign, evidence that Jesus was demanding Céline's future as a sacrifice. Her career as a nun would be a gift she made to God, rather than vice versa.

On September 14, 1894, Céline entered Carmel as a postulant and, the conflict at last resolved, felt immediately at peace. Mother Agnes, convinced that her sister's artistic training would be of use to the community, allowed her to bring her photographic equipment with her, both camera and developing materials. The indulgence was not by any means usual, but then it wasn't usual to have four siblings within one convent, or to have one of those blood sisters as mother superior while another subjected herself to the extraordinary rigors of sanctification.

Also outside of the normal and expected progress of events would be the destiny of those photographs Céline would make in the Carmel, images that would be scrutinized and reproduced too many times to count, copied onto postcards and calendars and coffee mugs, purchased even now, this very day, on street corners in Lisieux. Thérèse's face, its calm regard, is one we might imagine for a milkmaid – easy to picture her cheek resting against the warm flank of a cow as she worked to fill a bucket – but, even when the images are poorly reproduced, her eyes arrest us. Described as blue, described as gray, they look darker in photographs. They search and, in some shots, penetrate. Along with written testimony, journals, and letters, Céline's pictures of her sister contributed to the extraordinary cult of personality that formed in the years after Thérèse's death; they had their impact on her canonization.

Her naked, poised, and youthful countenance framed dramatically by her black veil; her calm, her self-possession, the manner in which she returns our stares without wavering from the shining path she sees before her, bright as sunlight on water – all these announce Thérèse as one of the elect. Unlike the posthumous portrait Céline would paint of her sister, the one that hides a face behind an emblem and that has contributed to the un-knowing of Thérèse, the photographs provide a means for those who doubt Thérèse to touch her wounds.

'I FOUND HER VOICE very much changed,' Marie Guérin wrote to Marie and Céline at the end of 1894, commenting on Thérèse's hoarseness. 'I spoke to Francis [her brother-in-law, Doctor la Neele] about her. For the moment there is nothing serious, but it can become so from one day to the next, and then there will be no longer any remedy.'

Thérèse had long assumed she would die young – she wished it for herself, reunion with mother and father as much as union with God – but it is hard to know when she began to perceive her own physical deterioration. Contemporary medical technique was unable to diagnose tuberculosis definitively in any but its advanced stages, and even then doctors often confused it with lung cancer or pneumonia. Mediated by a third party, Doctor la Neele's assessment was guarded. It betrayed the helplessness of his profession to effectively treat a disease that had only twelve years earlier been attributed to a germ, rather than to heredity or temperament, to poverty or vice, to 'almost any form of unconventional behavior,' all of which would still be blamed by the masses for decades to come.

Focused as she was on the significance of the minute – *everything is so big in religion* – Thérèse would have found no contradiction, only confluence and sublime alignment, between the purposes of the tubercle bacilli and their Creator. 'Don't worry about me,' she wrote Céline after la Neele visited the convent, 'I am not sick; on the contrary, I have iron health.' But she added a qualification her biographers have interpreted as prescient: 'God can break iron just like clay.'

Whatever Thérèse might not acknowledge, behind her older sisters' request at the end of December 1894 that she write about her childhood was their fear that she was dying, and that the stories she told of their youth together – 'all these detailed accounts that we find so interesting,' as Marie put it – would be lost. Like their mother, Thérèse was observant; she'd noticed and remembered what the others had not. In the past year she'd become the convent's unofficial poet, making gifts of verse to the other nuns for their feast days, to inspire or to cheer, to communicate without breaking the rule of silence. She was careful never to favor her own sisters, never to express her own preferences. But why, as the eldest Martin sister asked possessively, 'should she compose little poems to please everybody,' why should she spend herself on plays for recreation rather than functioning as the family historian?

At the end of January, Thérèse played Joan of Arc being martyred – the role she'd written with herself in mind – and was nearly burned when the scenery caught fire from spirit lamps used to illuminate the stage. We have Céline's pictures of her sister in makeshift armor and a dark wig, a chain wrapped around her wrists. She looks appropriately wan and pensive, a girl unjustly condemned to death, and she looks exhausted. At the end of each day, during the one hour allowed for individual recreation, Thérèse was writing in her cell, at first concerned that the task would 'distract [her] heart by too much concentration on [her]self' and thus impede her spiritual progress. But she'd learned to obey simply and without question. If an order came from a superior – in this case her sister, the prioress – then it must necessarily express the will of God. By the end of 1895, she'd filled six of the cheapest exercise books available (ten centimes apiece, thirty pages long); she'd completed the first and longest of the three manuscripts that would constitute her autobiography. She never revised or erased, she followed no outline, but wrote what came into her head as she sat on a stool and bent over the book, relying on Zélie's letters to begin her life at the beginning of her life, inventing herself in the voice of her mother.

Pauline could not have known consciously that it was a key moment for Thérèse to review her life in the faith. Along with her camera, Céline had brought notebooks with her, passages copied from the Old Testament, which Thérèse did not have in Carmel. (The Louvain Bible, the translation authorized for French Catholics, did not include an Old Testament.) In the notebooks Thérèse found a passage from Proverbs that struck with particular force: 'If anyone is a very little one, let him come to me.' Did this not confirm a downward path to exaltation? Reviewing her brief past, Thérèse could see her soul's direction and might anticipate its necessary steps.

Always in a hurry, now she was even more so. She'd read and even written of the great figures, those she called mountains of the faith, Saints Augustine and Paul, Venerable Joan. But she was a grain of sand, she was working on lowliness, hiddenness, invisibility. How did one measure such efforts?

Night after night, as she traced her development, Thérèse's heart was not distracted but informed. From earliest consciousness, she had wanted to be good, perfectly virtuous, but the only progress she made came through God. Each gain was not one of will – not even of a will as extraordinary as hers – but of love. Were the notebook entries dated, we could know exactly where in the story of her soul she had arrived during June of 1895. Assuming she worked steadily, at the even pace required by her schedule – an hour each night and no more – she would have written her way to the middle of what took her just a year to accomplish, the passage describing the Christmas 'miracle' when she felt 'charity enter into my soul, the need to forget myself and please others.' God's love had transformed her at the age of thirteen, unlocked the prison of self and morbid sensitivity. Was it a further meditation on that first and essential grace that inspired her Act of Oblation?

On June 9, 1895, during a mass celebrating the feast of the Holy Trinity, Thérèse had what she described as an awakening. Familiar with the idea of substitutive suffering, of offering oneself as a victim of God's judgment in order to free souls from purgatory, she had a sudden vision of herself as a different kind of victim. Immediately inflamed by her idea, she dragged Céline to Mother Agnes so they could ask the prioress's permission to offer themselves formally as 'sacrificial victims' to God's merciful love – love that was infinitely more demanding, more thoroughly immolating, than his justice. Pauline was hurrying to get letters in the mail and paid little attention to Thérèse, who was too overwrought to make herself clear. Céline remembered: 'The thing didn't seem important. Our mother said yes.'

In her cell, Thérèse drew up an 'Act of Oblation' for herself and for her sister, and on June 11, the two of them knelt before the Miraculous Virgin, and Thérèse read the document she had written and signed. Through Mary's intercession, she pledged herself and Céline to Jesus:

I ask You to come and take possession of my soul . . . consuming all my imperfections like the fire that transforms everything into itself. . . .

In the evening of this life, I shall appear before You with empty hands, for I do not ask You Lord to count my works. . . .

Time is nothing in Your eyes, and a single day is like a thousand years. You can, then, in one instant, prepare me to appear before You.

In order to live in one single act of perfect Love, I OFFER MYSELF AS A VICTIM OF HOLOCAUST TO YOUR MERCIFUL LOVE, asking You to consume me incessantly, allowing the waves of infinite tenderness shut up within You to overflow into my soul, and that thus I may become a martyr of Your Love, O my God!

May this martyrdom, after having prepared me to appear before You, finally cause me to die, and may my soul take its flight. . . .

The act, several pages long, moved through all the young nun's ardent hopes: she wanted to love God, to exist only for the glory of His church, to be no less than a saint. She could not bear separation from God; she asked that God take away her freedom to displease Him. She wanted to be consumed by divine love, to become one with its fire, eternally safe from separation. Beneath her plea, she signed her name, *Marie-Françoise-Thérèse of the Child Jesus and the Holy Face, unworthy Carmelite religious.*

Earnest, deadly earnest. Articulating what had long existed in her heart. Asking for what had already been granted: to be incessantly consumed.

ON JUNE 14, a few days after her oblation, Thérèse was in the choir, making the stations of the cross, when she was assailed by a burning sensation all over her body. 'I felt myself suddenly wounded by a flash of fire so intense I thought I would die,' she would tell Pauline during the last weeks of her life. At the time, however, the two sisters remained carefully on guard against familial affection. They barely discussed what Thérèse came to regard as the one moment of extraordinary grace in a religious life otherwise marked by God's silence and withdrawal. The taste of what she knew saints often experienced both excited and reassured her: the moment of rapture was a positive answer to her oblation, a little demonstration of what heavenly fire could do. Immediately, she began campaigning for her sister Marie and the novices in her charge to make the same act. But before anyone else could kneel and speak the words Thérèse had written, Mother Agnes had to share the oblation with a superior to make sure it made no theological missteps.

With minor changes it was accepted (not by Delatroëtte,

who had died on October 8, but by Father Lemonnier, who that month had preached the fall retreat), and the official sanction pleased Thérèse. Still, she didn't find others eager to pray for immolation, even if it was divine love that ignited the fire. She besieged Marie with intramural letters of encouragement, the gist of these being that such sacrifice wouldn't hurt – 'when we love a thing the pain disappears' – but while Marie eventually agreed to make the oblation, she was never able to desire what Thérèse desired. She wasn't her sister, possessed, as Marie described Thérèse, 'by God . . . absolutely possessed, just as the wicked are possessed by the devil.'

Thérèse was falling headlong into the flaming heart of Christ, while Léonie had once again faltered and left the convent in Caen, returning to Lisieux on July 20. She came to her four sisters in the Carmel parlor for a standard visit of one half-hour, timed by a sandglass, during which she wept without stopping, crying so hard, as Thérèse wrote her aunt Guérin, that they were unable to get even a word of explanation out of her. Isidore Guérin took his prodigal niece into his home, and she remained in his care until she returned, successfully, to the Visitation in 1899. Even when not overcome by tears, Léonie spoke little of her sufferings – she was best remembered for the remark 'Noblesse Oblige: I belong to a family of saints and must not stain the record.' But in 1895, thirty-two and still not able to find her way, she must have felt her shame and isolation intensely.

In October, Mother Agnes entrusted Thérèse with a brother

in the faith, an aspiring missionary named Maurice-Barthélémy Bellière, who had written the Carmel asking for a sister with whom he might correspond, on whom he could count for the support of prayers and sacrifices. In her state of chronic loneliness, her lifelong anguish of separation, Thérèse was excited by the gift, perhaps out of proportion. Abbé Bellière was only just twenty-one and unsure of his future. After a first rapturous exchange of letters, Thérèse received a note from Bellière saying, bluntly, that he was entering military service. She heard no more from him until the following July, but she continued to pray for him, just as she remained faithful to all her personal projects: her work with the novices, the family memoir she had promised Pauline, and her poems, twenty-five by now, some of them quite long.

For Céline, who had countered Thérèse's suggestion that she offer herself as a victim of love with a request for a poem enumerating all the sacrifices Céline had already made for God, Thérèse came up with a thirty-three-stanza life of Christ, which she titled 'Jesus, My Beloved, Remember!' Based on the Gospels, it did not celebrate what Céline had done for God but called Jesus' attention to all He had suffered for Céline, and returned over and over to the theme of Christ's humility:

> Remember that you wandered as a Stranger on earth.
> You, The Eternal Word,
> You had nothing . . . no, not even a stone

Céline would recall 'astonishment' at this gift, a negative rather than positive surprise, it would seem from the admission that it was 'only later that [she] understood how right

[her] little sister was' to rebuke her in verse.

Others of Thérèse's literary efforts were also not appreciated. As novice mistress, she wrote a short and simple entertainment for Christmas of 1895 and spent more energy and attention on a play in honor of Pauline's feast day, January 21. 'The Flight into Egypt,' based on a legendary story of the Holy Family's encounter with a band of robbers, was in fact so long that Mother Agnes stopped the performance before it was over and scolded Thérèse for taking too much of the community's time. Thérèse succumbed to tears, but perhaps they flowed from a compound grief. The night before, she'd presented Pauline with the completed memoirs of her childhood, and her sister had put the manuscript away without reading it and without seeing what Thérèse had painstakingly designed and copied onto the final page: her own and Jesus' 'coats of arms,' linked by a verse – 'Love is repaid by love alone' – taken from Saint John of the Cross. Each blazon is filled with images that Thérèse herself decoded, lest Pauline miss any significance. Christ is represented by a vine ('I am the vine and you are the branches') as well as by paintings of the Holy Face, the Infant Jesus, a triangle (Trinity), and the morning star. The trajectory of Thérèse's soul is seen in a cluster of grapes offered to the Baby Jesus, a harp singing of love, a white lily, a weak reed, and a palm of martyrdom.

Although she was disappointed by Pauline's seeming indifference to her labors, it had become impossible for Thérèse to resent any form of rejection: she was too eager for any chance to share in the bitter experience of God, who had Himself been rejected.

*

Lent arrived with its usual schedule of deprivations. In March, the order's sixteen chapter nuns (those who voted) reelected Marie de Gonzague as prioress but required seven ballots to reach a majority decision. Unlike Mother Agnes, Mother Marie did not offer the novitiate to her runner-up; instead she suggested Thérèse become the official novice mistress, a title Thérèse refused, even though she continued as the primary teacher and adviser to the newer members of the community. Thérèse would meet with five novices now, including her sister Céline and her cousin Marie, who had left home for Carmel even as Léonie had stepped in to fill her place as daughter in the Guérin home.

On Holy Thursday, April 2, 1896, nearly a year after she had made her oblation to love, Thérèse extinguished the light in her cell and lay down on her pallet. She had felt well enough during the past weeks to observe the Lenten fast 'in all its rigor.' That night she'd participated in the vigil at the altar, awaiting the holiest day of the year, the day on which death dies and the Bridegroom is resurrected. Within minutes of getting into bed, she was aware of a 'bubbling stream mounting to [her] lips,' a warm flow of what she assumed was blood but did not allow herself to confirm. The inconvenient lamp, the lamp she called 'ours,' not 'mine,' was already snuffed, its wick lowered by means of a pin. To relight it for purposes of self-indulgence would amount to a failure of discipline. Thérèse held her soaked, sticky handkerchief in her hand and waited for sunrise.

Most young women, even a morbidly romantic one, would be frightened by the prospect of a pulmonary hemorrhage. If she chose to wait for the morning's corroboration of a death sentence, it would be out of denial, even terror, the hope of not having to spend so dark a night alone. Thérèse betrayed no fear, at least not on the page, not in retrospect. Until this point in her life, her faith had been unquestioning, airtight. She understood her parents' protracted deaths as spiritually precocious and economical: Zélie and Louis had satisfied the demands of purgatory while still on earth. Did Thérèse allow her excitement over the idea that exile from God, from mother and father, might be at last drawing to an end distract her from a less attractive possibility: that her most intense suffering might be just beginning? We cannot know. 'Nothing is less spontaneous than a letter, nothing less transparent than an autobiography, which is designed to conceal as much as it reveals.' Thérèse's measured words do not make her readers into witnesses. In her – *our* – cell, she was alone; more than a year would pass before she wrote: 'I thought that perhaps I was going to die and my soul was flooded with joy.'

Upon waking she took the handkerchief to the window. What she saw 'filled [her] with a great consolation.' It was of course significant to her that Christ announced her imminent death on Good Friday, the anniversary of his own crucifixion.

Virginal milk, tender breast.
White wings, chaste dove, seraphic lyre.
Tears, sweet exile, brave warrior, little shepherd girl.
Lamb. Lily. Daisy. Rose.
Burning arrow, burn me away until nothing is left.

LOUIS MARTIN may have cloistered his daughters, protecting them from those aspects of secular culture he considered vulgar and dangerous to their moral development, but he didn't – couldn't – separate them from the popular imagery of the time in which they lived. Poems written by Thérèse prove her familiarity with the symbols and sentiments of the romantic tradition. To suggest innocence, she used a lamb; for sacrifice, a plucked flower. To speak of divine love, she had only the language of mortal sentiment. Limited as a poet, so was she as a human being. Much as she despised the flesh, she was incarnate. What were the material means of consecrating oneself to love?

'It was the fashion to suffer from the lungs,' Alexandre Dumas *père* remembered. 'Everyone was consumptive, poets especially; it was good form to spit blood after each emotion that was at all sensational, and to die before reaching the age of thirty.' The tubercular 'look,' pale and wasted with feverish eyes, was a standard of beauty, and of femininity. How could a daughter of Zélie Martin, who complained that she and her daughters were helpless 'slaves to fashion,' have hoped to escape so powerful a vogue, one that had swept Europe and America and even surfaced in novels of the Far East?

In a French town of 1896, tuberculosis was inescapable, both as contagion and as metaphor. Zélie's sister, whom Thérèse visited at the Visitation in Caen, had died of it; Sister Marie-Antoinette, Carmel's thirty-five-year-old extern nun, was consumptive and would die that year. Even if Thérèse never read Hugo's *Les Misérables* or Alcott's *Little Women* (published serially in France in 1878 and as a book in 1880), even though she had no opportunity to see a production of Dumas's *La Dame aux camélias* or the opera based on Murger's *Scènes de la vie de bohème*, she was no less receptive to the romantic idea of redemptive suffering that tuberculosis offered.

Appropriated by writers and artists, the consumptive heroine, the woman who dies of a love so transcendently pure that it burns away its mortal vessel, was the collective invention of an age. Prefigured for centuries by the same paragons who compelled Thérèse – the Church had always associated the destruction of the flesh with the strengthening of the spirit – the specifically tubercular martyrdom grew out of the nineteenth century's attributing consumption to refinement and spirituality, to ardor rather than germs. Tubercle bacilli infected both genders equally, but tuberculosis was understood as a feminine, and feminizing, disease, the uncontrolled bleeding of pulmonary hemorrhage imaginatively linked not only to crucifixion but to menstruation, an unclean flow that represented both fertility and the corruptible nature of woman, her inherent need to be purified.

For Thérèse, who grew up denying her physical self, the 'flesh that cannot be tamed and therefore must be obliterated,' an unconscious conflation of the two distinct kinds of bleeding would have been even more potent. Having never allowed the expression of her sexuality, she granted it a power and danger that was absolute, irresistible. A single kiss, she imagined, would be sufficient to make her a 'Magdalene'; if Carmel hadn't taken her at fifteen, her alternative plan had been to run away to the Gomorrah of Paris, where she would live in a halfway home, among fallen women. The Church, in its preoccupation with original sin, encouraged even the most chaste women to identify themselves with Eve, convinced them of their need for sanctification. What difference was there between Thérèse and Dumas's Marguerite Gautier, the courtesan who discovered true, selfless love and died of it? Thérèse would not have perceived any.

With heightened energy – a 'fervor' – granted by this 'first call' from her Bridegroom, Thérèse assisted at Prime and the Chapter of Pardons, a Good Friday tradition in which each nun sought absolution from her sisters. She later recalled being 'transported' by her new, secret happiness. The Rule did not allow a nun to conceal physical illness from her mother superior, and in what reads as a spasm of masochistic excitement, she told Mother Marie of her hemorrhage and asked to be allowed to fulfill all the remaining Lenten obligations. She wasn't in pain, she insisted, so why not? Astonishingly, Mother Marie agreed, and so Thérèse fasted and did her chores, stood on a ladder in a cold draft, and washed windows.

Discipline, routine, obedience to a higher order. In spas and sanatoria across Europe, consumptive patients submitted to a rule, a life punctuated by the ringing of bells. They rose on schedule, ate in a common refectory, submitted to examination by medical officers, exercised or not as prescribed, took their temperatures, endured compulsory periods of silence, turned out their lights on time and slept as directed. Like all good religious, they pinned hope of salvation on obedience.

The next night, April 3, Good Friday, Thérèse hemorrhaged again. Doctor la Neele examined her as much as he was able by putting his head through the oratory grille and auscultating through the layers of her habit. Surely she did not describe the hemoptyses to the doctor as she did later on the page – a *'bubbling stream'* of blood – because he made the comforting diagnosis of a burst blood vessel in her throat and allowed her to continue to work as if nothing serious had happened. Throat sprays and camphor salves were prescribed, remedies that the patient happily assumed useless.

And yet, after so dramatic an announcement, the resumption of normalcy, even a requested normalcy, was discouraging. Thérèse hoped for immediate death, but she would get an agonizingly slow one, eighteen months of martyrdom without glory, without the solace of faith. Not that she wavered in her beliefs, but she felt nothing: Jesus announced himself to her and withdrew.

DURING THOSE 'very joyful days of the Easter season' that followed on the annunciation of the hemorrhages, Thérèse was abruptly plunged into what she called 'the thickest darkness.' The faith she had always taken for granted – 'living,' 'clear,' uninterrupted by doubt – vanished, leaving her in a despair so profound it defied articulation. Once, she had found words inadequate to the 'secrets of heaven'; now she discovered they were useless when trying to describe what seemed a visit to hell. Evocative, if not as precise or accurate as she would have liked, was her analogy of an obliterating fog, so thick that she could not conceive of light, could no longer imagine God's presence.

Thérèse's temptation against faith, as she understood it, persisted without relief until the end of her life. Writing what became the last chapters of her autobiography, she observed that her 'little story which resembled a fairy tale is all of a sudden changed into a prayer.' Twenty-three, without expectation of completing her twenty-fourth year, without hearth or husband or child, without the solace of even one friend – for

Thérèse had sacrificed the selfish preferences of friendship to the indiscriminate embrace of charity, just as she'd abandoned her beloved biological father for an invisible celestial suitor – Thérèse Martin had invested every hope in her vocation. What if, now that she was dying, there was no heaven?

With a courage hidden by determined cheer, the conviction that she must protect the community from her doubts, Thérèse accepted her new terror as she accepted every other spiritual trial, as the will of God, who must have found her at last strong enough to experience the misery of the unbeliever. For this was the only consolation she could draw from her unhappiness. Even meditation on the love of Christ offered no solace:

> When I want to rest my heart fatigued by the darkness that surrounds it by the memory of the luminous country after which I aspire, my torment redoubles; it seems to me that the darkness, borrowing the voice of sinners, says mockingly to me: 'You are dreaming about the light, about a fatherland embalmed in the sweetest of perfumes; you are dreaming about the eternal possession of the Creator of all these marvels; you believe that one day you will walk out of this fog that surrounds you! Advance, advance; rejoice in death which will give you not what you hope for but a night still more profound, the night of nothingness.'

If, up to this point in her story, it has been possible to dismiss Thérèse as a spiritual model of limited use or appeal, as *little* because she had never been tempted, these eleventh-hour confessions, never voiced earlier in her life, correct any such assumptions. Once she had found her initial, *T*, written in the sky, God's invitation and blessing spelled out for all the world to see; now she saw 'a wall which reaches right up to the heavens and covers the starry firmament.' As painful as it is to witness her desolation, the preceding passage – anguished, unflinching – excites as much as it troubles Thérèse's readers. At last she has taken her place among us, not so much revealed herself as human as given birth to her naked self, plummeting to earth, wet and new and terrified. If we allow her to become a saint, if we believe in her, it's because here, finally, she has achieved mortality.

Assailed by silence and emptiness, afraid of what she'd committed to the page – 'I don't want to write any longer about it; I fear I might blaspheme; I fear even that I have already said too much' – Thérèse earned her place among the moderns, anticipating the existential accusation of Sartre:

You see the void above our heads? That is God. You see this hole in the ground? That's what God is. You see this crack in the door? That's God too. Silence is God. Absence is God. God is human loneliness.

Convinced that her doubts were evil, Thérèse shared them with no one. She wrote cheerful notes to Léonie and to her novices; she dreamed up a long allegory for Mother Marie de Gonzague to help her superior see convent politics in heaven's light; she fired off chatty letters that made light of her family's worries over her health. 'I shall allow the famous Doctor de Cornière to speak, to whom I had the *distinguished honor* of being presented yesterday in the speakroom,' she wrote her aunt. 'This illustrious personage, after having *honored* me with a look, declared that I looked well!' she exclaimed with perhaps too evident irony; the report could hardly have reassured Madame Guérin. De Cornière was 'famous' in that he was the official doctor for the community, summoned not to examine Thérèse but to attend to the more imminently dying Sister Marie-Antoinette, compared with whom Thérèse might have appeared 'well' in the context of an abbreviated greeting. But no matter how she looked, Thérèse placed no faith in doctors, privately dismissing their diagnoses as the work of unenlightened people who devoted themselves to the very aspect of existence that ought to be despised, ignored, defeated.

Answering her fears with work and prayer, she developed a wry, even black, sense of humor. Almost never did she break down and allude to her spiritual trial. 'If only you knew,' she admitted to the sacristan, 'what darkness I am plunged into! . . . Everything has disappeared on me, and I am left with love alone.'

'When I sing of the happiness of heaven,' she confided to Mother Marie, 'I feel no joy. . . . I sing simply what I want to believe.'

In her own estimation, Thérèse made more acts of faith during the last year of her illness than she had throughout her entire previous life. Despair, as all religious knew, was infectious, dangerous. Tuberculosis – which by November would have finished off Sister Marie-Antoinette – was a matter of constitution, of fate, the will of God.

Where was Thérèse in the course of her illness? As readers of

Victorian novels know, pulmonary tuberculosis typically follows a chronic and protracted course. Infection with the bacilli, generally inhaled in the form of droplets of sputum, might precede active consumption by years, because the germs, tiny and slow to multiply, cause little damage at first and no symptoms. It takes a few months for tissue to become sensitive to the invading cells and for inflammation to result. Tubercles form around the clusters of bacilli in an attempt to isolate the infection within. These lesions either rupture, spreading the disease and leaving holes in the lung cavity, or calcify into nodules. By the spring of 1894, when Thérèse had been troubled by sore throats and hoarseness, the disease would have been well established. Two years later, with the first hemorrhages, her lung tissue had been irreparably damaged. Now she began to be troubled by coughing fits that prevented her from sleeping, which in turn contributed to the depressive effects of serious illness.

Month after month, she persevered without relief from her 'temptations against the faith.' No longer proud, but no less stubborn, she waited for God. Consolation came, on May 9, in the form of a dream, one she remembered well enough to record in detail four months later. The dream was exceptionally clear and vivid, of that type the dreamer perceives as more real than waking experience. Thérèse found herself in a gallery with several other nuns and the prioress when three Carmelites, their faces hidden under veils, approached. It was clear to her that these unknown sisters came from heaven, and Thérèse wanted very much to see their faces. No sooner was she was aware of this unvoiced, fervent desire than the tallest of the three advanced and lifted her veil. She covered

Thérèse with its layers, enveloping the two of them underneath, and revealed herself as Anne of Jesus, the foundress of the French Carmel, who died in 1621. The fact that Thérèse was, as she put it, *'absolutely indifferent to Venerable Mother Anne'* convinced Thérèse of the dream's validity. Why conjure a vision of a personage for whom she felt so little?

'Her face was beautiful but with an immaterial beauty . . . suffused with an unspeakably gentle light, a light . . . produced from within.' The description is typical of apparitions of the Virgin and recalls Thérèse's childhood vision of Mary, possessing the same transcendent beauty, a light that 'suffused' the face, conveying unearthly love. The echo was not unconscious. Thérèse concluded that the dream – the visitation – marked the anniversary of the earlier apparition, 'the second SUNDAY of Mary's month,' she wrote.

Seeing Anne's look of pure love and feeling the sweetness of her 'caresses,' Thérèse beseeched the Madonna-like vision to relieve her of some of the agonies she'd been suffering. Would God leave her for a long time on earth, she wanted to know, or would He come soon to get her? 'Soon, soon, I promise you,' Anne reassured. Was there anything left for her to accomplish, or was God content with His servant? Thérèse pressed, not asking the more direct questions: Why was God silent, unreachable? Was it because she had somehow failed to please Him?

'The saint's face took on an expression incomparably more tender,' and she told Thérèse that God was well pleased with his servant. He wanted 'no other thing.' Anne embraced Thérèse 'with more love than the tenderest of mothers has ever given to her child.' As when Thérèse had been ten years old, ill and despairing, so now was she comforted by her vision of a luminous and accepting and all-powerful mother. She might feel herself deserted, but this was a defect of her imperfect human perception: she would not be abandoned, either to mortal suffering or to the abyss of eternal separation, the nothingness that tormented her while awake.

Aside from the gift of this one dream, and 'at times a very small ray,' Thérèse found her days as long as suffering could make them. She would not ask to be relieved of any task, no matter how arduous; she attended every devotion; she drove herself to the end of her strength. Under the cloak of pretty phrases and sweet optimism was a will that frightened those around Thérèse, her sisters and the one or two other nuns who watched her carefully enough to see the exhaustion she tried to hide. Her obedience, as all who testified during the beatification process made clear, was perfect; she accepted every directive as the Word of God.

Reading Thérèse's account of the months following the Easter hemorrhages, one is tempted to apply the words *folie à deux* to the always complicated and sometimes destructive relationship between Thérèse and Marie de Gonzague, who appears in a role opposite to that of Anne of Jesus: the withholding mother, the one who did not rush to tell Thérèse that she could relax, that she could trust in God's love if not her own goodness.

In compliance with the Rule, Thérèse had immediately reported her hemorrhages, but it was the letter rather than the spirit of the law that she served. She refused to consider the increasing frailty of her body, on which she turned with renewed hostility, not appalled or fearful but thrilled by its wasting. She, who claimed little advantage could come from mortification of the flesh, conspired with her prioress to create a new and rarefied – a spiritual – sanatorium, a set of living conditions that gave every advantage to the disease, stripped every support from its victim.

'How much I am touched by all your material attention. Ah! Believe it, Mother, the heart of your child is filled with gratitude, and never will she forget what she owes you,' Thérèse wrote the prioress, words tempting to reread and even speak aloud in order to discover the exact emphasis, the voice in which they might have been uttered, had they been uttered. Is there any irony here, any cloaked accusation? Again and again – too many times? – Thérèse gave thanks for 'the dew of humiliation,' for Mother Marie's having 'never spared' her. Indeed, she was indebted to the prioress, to anyone who so effectively pushed her toward martyrdom, but can't we detect at least wistfulness beneath the 'gratitude'? Another sort of indulgence, different and gentler, might have been welcomed.

In what seems acknowledgment of her subject's imminent departure, in July Céline took a number of photographs of Thérèse, posed alone rather than among the other members of the community. Self-conscious in the manner of the period, still they possess the immediate nostalgia of family snapshots, stealing a moment out of time even as they acknowledge the relentlessness of time, magnifying the obsession with death and impermanence that was central to the Martins' personal culture as well as to the greater Catholic milieu. And, of course, they provide a voyeuristic thrill uncommon to the era: they mark the material progress of tuberculosis, the destruction of the flesh that was inextricable from the mysterious, spiritual alchemy that made this mortal into an immortal.

In one, Thérèse embraces the base of the towering crucifix she could see from her cell, the one in the middle of the cloister garden. Her right hand holds a branch of lilies against the nailed feet of Christ, her left is wrapped tightly around the cross itself, her eyes are cast upward. The effect, on the whole, is one of shipwreck, of sinking rather than expectation. A second pose, more often reproduced, shows Thérèse standing in the sacristy, again holding the branch of lilies, holding it firmly in both hands as if it were a tool rather than a spray of flowers, her eyes on her viewers. She looks amused, almost. Her small, prim mouth resists an actual smile, and her eyes suppress merriment: she is party to a wonderful secret. In a third, Thérèse rests against the low cloister wall, lilies beside her. It is not possible to decide whether she looks at or beyond us – perhaps both, for her expression, stern, gentle, sorrowful, is genuinely Christ-like. She holds a book, a gift from a young priest, Adolphe Roulland, and a scroll bearing words from her namesake, Teresa of Ávila: 'I would give a thousand lives just to save one soul!'

Roulland, a seminarian from Paris, came to the Carmel that summer. He celebrated mass at the convent and spoke at length with Thérèse, whose connection to him was immediate and natural. Through this 'Brother,' she would experience a life she found as attractive as it was impossible: that of the foreign missionary. When Roulland left for China in August, he carried with him ten of what Thérèse considered her best poems, including one composed for his 'exile' in China, a romantic effort linking her own 'sacrifice in Carmel' with his in 'East Szechuan,' and signed 'The little sister of a Missionary.'

Over the next year, Thérèse would exchange a number of long letters with her two spiritual brothers, Roulland and Abbé Bellière, who had suddenly resurfaced, asking for prayers to save him from the military life. 'Tear me away from it at all costs. . . . Or I am lost,' he begged, and she responded with sincere fervor. Her prayers for herself might be met with silence, but at least there were two young men – representatives of Christ – who counted her petitions as valuable and placed their vocations in her hands. When two hundred 'pagans' were converted in 'Ho-pau-tchung,' Roulland credited Thérèse's prayers with having 'drawn down the grace of God.'

And not only Père Roulland and Abbé Bellière counted her prayers as indispensable. In 1927, Thérèse, who left Normandy only once (and then in order to secure her imprisonment in a convent in Lisieux), would be made patron of the universal missions, an honor she shared with the well-traveled Saint Francis Xavier, entombed in Goa, on the Malabar Coast of India.

In September, on the eve of Thérèse's annual private retreat, her eldest sister, Marie of the Sacred Heart, asked her for what would become the second of the three manuscripts that make up her autobiography. Marie had probably read the account of family life that Thérèse had written for Pauline, because she seems to have seen some gaps that needed filling. 'This is perhaps your last retreat,' Marie observed. As such it presented an opportune moment for her precocious godchild to write down her 'little doctrine.'

Thérèse had been reading Proverbs and Psalms, Isaiah's vision of blind faith, of a benevolent savior who will 'sweep away transgressions like a cloud.' Redemption was based on love, not works. Knowing this, still she struggled to reconcile her boundless desire to serve God, to accomplish 'the most heroic deeds,' to be 'warrior, priest, doctor, apostle, martyr,' with circumstances that would seem to prevent it. During her retreat, she sifted again through Paul's first letter to the Corinthians.

'Are all apostles? Are all prophets? Are all teachers?' Paul asks. 'If I give away all I have, and if I deliver my body to be burned, but have not love, I gain nothing.'

Genius of renunciation, Thérèse had given everything away; she had delivered her body to be burned. The final step, then, the answer to existential nothingness, to darkness, fog, despair, and silence, was love. 'Love never ends; as for prophecies, they will pass away; as for tongues, they will cease; as for knowledge, it will pass away.'

Love.

Mysticism presents like a Möbius strip: a simple path and yet one that twists, inverts, and greets itself, no end, no beginning. Thérèse must have read 1 Corinthians many times before; now, in a flash of illumination, one that made her 'a child of light,' she finally understood, she 'found what she was seeking by always stooping down.' The letter she wrote her sister is filled with underscores and exclamation points, her tidy handwriting charged with excitement, emphatic, energetic, slanting forward in the old manner, then abruptly vertical again.

> Oh luminous Beacon of love, I know how to reach You, I have found the secret. . . . I am only a child, powerless and weak, and yet it is my weakness that gives me the boldness of offering myself. . . . Yes, in order that Love be fully satisfied, it is necessary that it lower itself, and that it lower itself into nothingness, and transform this nothingness into fire.
>
> Oh Jesus, I know it, love is repaid by love alone.

Throughout the coming year, a year of increasing pain and humiliations caused not by the prioress this time but by her own body, a year of God's silence, His seeming abandonment, Thérèse would remain 'a child of light.' She would live in love; she would not betray her epiphany. To her sisters in Carmel, she may have seemed the same as she always was: as selfless and polite, as generous with her time and attention. Internally, she had a new battle to fight with herself. Beyond the elementary spiritual exercises of seeking out the company of the most objectionable nun or hunting through the attic for the most inconvenient tools, now her task was 'not allowing one little sacrifice to escape, not one look, one word, profiting by all the smallest things and doing them by love.'

Martyrdom wasn't one act, or even a collection of actions, it was perhaps nothing that could be measured – perceived – by mortals. Rather, it was what Flannery O'Connor called a 'habit of being.' Thérèse intended to leave herself nothing, not a thought or a sigh, that wasn't consecrated to God. Here was her mystical union with Christ, here she disappeared into the heart of the Church, for whom 'the smallest act of pure Love is of more value than all other works together' – *smallest* perhaps deceptive here, in the same way that the word *little* can mislead when Thérèse applies it to herself, because Love is not measurable, except in its purity, and human judgment, the measure of human accomplishment, is useless, even counterproductive. As Thérèse observed in a letter to Sister Marie of Saint Joseph, the nun with whom she worked in the linen room, 'the most *painful*, the most LOVING martyrdom' is that which goes unnoted by mortals, the martyrdom of the heart that 'Jesus alone sees.'

Thérèse was on the other side of a private, internal revolution, like that of her Christmas conversion, an awakening that alienated her from the rest of the community, including her sisters.

'I dread all that you love,' Marie responded to the treatise she'd requested from Thérèse. She understood that God looked upon Thérèse's desires as 'works,' sacrifices Marie herself was unwilling to make. Marie would not dismantle the boundaries of her own psyche in order to give all of herself to God.

In what seems a spasm of denial, Thérèse made plans to travel to the Carmel in Saigon, the capital city of French Indochina. She was excited by letters from Père Roulland, who had at last reached China and who described local customs with charming detail, rendering inconvenience picturesque and quaint. En route to his posting in Szechuan, Roulland had visited the Saigon mission and now relayed the prioress's request for personnel. Might this be a providential sign? Thérèse was enjoying a remission of symptoms; and, undoubtedly, she was fleeing the idea of sharing the fate of Sister Marie-Antoinette, who died on November 4. She hung a map of Szechuan on the wall, where she could see it as she worked.

The baking of altar bread provided a source of income for the Lisieux Carmel, and from the convent, Roullard received a box of large hosts that he kept in his room, 'ready to embark once more.' If the work of her hands, as well as her prayers, accompanied her brother, could she not go east, too? In November the community offered a novena to the martyr Théophane Vénard, who had been beheaded in Tonkin, Southeast Asia, in 1861. The sisters of Carmel asked for a sign of God's will: Could Thérèse travel east? Before the nine days of prayer were finished, she began coughing once more; her brief period of apparent health was over.

A letter dated December 4, 1896, from Sister Marie of the Eucharist to her father, Isidore Guérin, described the cell of Thérèse. Usually, nuns did not enter each other's rooms, but Thérèse was ill enough to sometimes take meals apart from the others gathered in the refectory. Perhaps it was Marie who had carried up to Thérèse the gift of a dish of veal and mushrooms, sent by the Guérins, who were in the habit of providing strengthening meals to the sick of Carmel. 'Picture to yourself a real hovel,' Marie wrote, 'the plaster walls scratched and blackened, a poor mean litter – this is the only word for it . . . covered with her old clothes that served her as blankets.'

To offset the intensifying cold, Thérèse was permitted – directed – by the prioress to use a foot warmer in her cell, but she made use of it only when she was forced to do so, submitting to temperatures 'inexorably causing her death,' in the opinion of Céline. She was giving Thérèse rubdowns with a 'hair cloth,' mortifications prescribed for her condition, along with vesicatories, the same burning mustard plasters Zélie had found too 'frightening' to alleviate Thérèse's childhood ailments. Vesicatories intentionally blistered the skin in order to stimulate circulation and promote healing in the proximate tissue of the lung. The treatments didn't work, but they had some value to Thérèse; they gave her an opportunity to submit obediently to pain she might offer as a sacrifice to God's love – love she sometimes described as tender and maternal but which, in her letter to Marie, she evoked by means of violent and predatory images.

Jesus is the bright and burning 'Sun of Love,' the 'Divine Eagle,' Thérèse a weak 'little bird,' incapable of flight, assailed by storms and surrounded by 'vultures' and 'demons.' 'Fascinated' by the 'eternal' eagle, she waited to become 'prey.' 'One day I hope that You, the Adorable Eagle, will come to fetch me, Your Little Bird; and ascending with it [*sic*] to the Furnace of Love, You will plunge it for all eternity into the burning Abyss of this Love to which it has offered itself as victim.'

On a more playful but still punishing note, on Christmas Eve Thérèse wrote to her novice Sister Marie of the Trinity that she might consider herself as a playing top for Jesus, one that required 'whipping' with a cord to make it spin. 'When I have been well entertained by you,' Thérèse imagined Jesus saying, 'I will take you up above and we shall play without any suffering.'

Perhaps, having removed all internal clutter, having made herself an empty chamber, Thérèse found it too awful to hear nothing but the echo of her own prayers. Better to conjure a voice of caprice – of a Divine Boy who might tear the wings from a fly – than allow God to remain silent.

Three days after Christmas, for the feast of the Holy Innocents, Thérèse composed a poem dedicated to her four brothers and sisters who had died in infancy. 'You were offered to God / As first fruits,' she wrote, betraying a certain wistful envy. Not only had her siblings been joined to their mother while Thérèse endured the 'bitter sadness' of exile, but they were spared the worries that consumed their dying sister. 'O astonishing privilege! / Without fighting you achieved the glory / Of conquerors.' As always, she voiced what she wanted to believe, that works were nothing compared with love, and yet as death approached, she betrayed anxiety that works were perhaps valuable.

In the midst of the sisters' singing Thérèse's new composition, Mother Marie de Gonzague lost her temper, observing tartly that such attention would only increase Thérèse's pride. The performance was cut short; but Thérèse didn't cry as she had when similarly rebuked by Pauline. It would seem that the prioress had provided an unintended kindness, temporary relief from internal conflict. Thérèse could always be grateful for humiliation, a sacrifice to offer to Christ, a means toward union.

On January 2, 1897, Thérèse Martin turned twenty-four. A letter to Pauline, dated January 9, offers the first explicit reference to her anticipated death. Others, to other correspondents, would follow. The romance of death – of martyrdom – was not peculiar to Thérèse; it filled the writings of her sisters and her missionary brothers. 'I want only to send you some relics of a future martyr,' Père Roulland wrote in February, enclosing a lock of his hair in the same letter. 'At the moment we are not in important danger of death,' he conceded, 'but from one day to the next we can receive thrusts from the knife.' Roulland's descriptions of banditry, famine, even cannibalism – a young man 'seized, strangled and cooked in a pot' – of Christians forced to hide themselves in mountain caves, must have provided as much cause for frustration as entertainment to the young woman huddled on a straw pallet in an unadorned cell. Above Thérèse's head, on the lintel of her cell's door, were the words *Jésus est mon unique Amour* (Jesus is my only Love), a message Thérèse scratched into the wood in her distinctive vertical script, probably during her last winter, when she spent so many hours fantasizing about the East.

Increasingly 'interested and touched' by the life of Théophane Vénard, whose biography she read in the wake of Père Roulland's departure for China, Thérèse began petitioning the young martyr for courage. Vénard, a priest from the foreign missions in Paris, was beheaded at the age of thirty-one in Hanoi. For two months before his death, he lived in a cage, writing letters filled with joy, anticipating what he likened to the cutting of a spring flower in the master's garden. Vénard went to this executioner singing, and as her last conversations with her sisters reveal, Thérèse identified fervently with this male blossom she had discovered. She found him 'very ordinary,' a man 'who loved his family very much,' who was cheerful, humble, and devoted to the Virgin. His was a 'little' soul like her own, and she kept a portrait of him near her, looked at it, spoke to it, caressed it. In the image, the young priest pointed a finger up toward heaven, offering the same gesture – the same promise of reunion in heaven – as had her father on the last occasion Thérèse saw him.

On February 2, she wrote a poem to Vénard, one of the few that she composed spontaneously. 'Soldier of Christ,' she called to him, 'Lend me your weapons.' She wanted, like Vénard, to win souls, but even more she needed the inspiration of what she assumed was his certainty. Weapons were the theme of her next composition as well, written in honor of the profession of her cousin Marie Guérin, on March 25.

I have put on the weapons of the All Powerful.
His divine hand has deigned to adorn me.
Hence forth nothing causes me alarm.

What were the weapons of the Carmelite? Poverty, chastity, obedience: Thérèse exhorted her cousin to gird herself with sacrifice; then she would be 'invincible,' she could 'face the fury of all hell' and be sure of victory. Of course it was Thérèse herself at war, battling with the evil of her doubts, determined to remain to the end of her life a true bride of Christ, 'smiling' in the face of fire, 'singing' as she died.

Lent began on March 3, and Thérèse tried to fast. She undertook a novena to Saint Francis Xavier, asking that she be allowed her missionary vocation, to be accomplished after her death. She would 'spend her heaven doing good on earth.' Her cousin Marie Guérin had been her last novice, whose profession meant that Thérèse had completed the earthly task she took most seriously. What remained was to die, a work she would achieve so well that it would secure her earthly fame.

A letter to Isidore Guérin, dated April 4, made clear that Thérèse's health had begun to deteriorate more quickly. She had a fever every afternoon and was sometimes so weak that even standing was impossible. Apparently, the disease had spread to her intestines, for she had no appetite; when she forced herself to eat she suffered indigestion and spells of vomiting. Six months remained of her life, months that would be documented exhaustively by photographs, letters, the final chapters of her autobiography, a handful of poems, and her 'last conversations.' Some members of the community might have regarded Sister Thérèse of the Infant Jesus as unremarkable, but her family was sufficiently convinced of her holiness to take notes for posterity. Pauline, Marie, Céline, and their cousin Marie settled in to a protracted deathwatch, each armed with notebook and pen.

IT'S TEMPTING, for the hagiographer, to begin with death rather than birth, to work backward from the more significant and conscious portal of earthly life. Death is the arena for sainthood, the testing ground. Youthful indulgence, sexual profligacy, all sins, from the venial to the deadly, are excused – welcomed – as a prelude to sanctity. Consider the case of one of Thérèse's 'mountains,' Augustine: jealous playboy, lying vandal, pagan infidel.

But not when he died. A saint's death must be holy, and Thérèse, watching herself, knew that others were watching her as well. Suffocation, starvation, gangrene: she embraced each new agony as sacrifice, another way to love. She gave herself no opportunity for grief or anger or even impatience.

Pauline, the most thorough of Thérèse's self-appointed witnesses, secured permission from Mother Marie to visit and speak with Thérèse when she was confined in her cell. If Pauline didn't suspect the significance of her 'yellow notebook' to strangers, hadn't foreseen that the dialogue therein would be examined during Thérèse's beatification process, still she had read her sister's account of their childhood together, and she knew how invaluable Zélie's correspondence had been to the family after they lost her living voice. There were compelling personal motives to capture as much of Thérèse as possible while she was 'still in our midst.' Too, family outside of the cloister would have no opportunity to speak with her directly, and Léonie had already written Céline asking if it wouldn't be possible to transcribe everything Thérèse said, adding how much comfort it would give her to have that contact, that sense of nearness to her sister.

By April, Thérèse was coughing blood again, and she began, bit by bit, to withdraw from participation in community life. Relieved of heavy chores, she continued to work in the linen room, sewing and mending, but found it less and less possible to recite the Divine Office in the choir. She hadn't much breath to walk, let alone sing, but she resisted making any concession to her increasing weakness: after all, she had the indelible example of her mother's death, and Zélie had carried on until she collapsed. Thérèse forced herself to go to recreation and hid whatever she could from the community – successfully enough that some of the sisters grumbled about indulgences granted to a nun who wasn't really all that sick – but in fact she was often close to fainting. She admitted to one of her novices that 'it took me more than half an hour to get up to our cell, I had to sit down on almost every step of the stairs to get my breath. When I finally reached our cell, I had to make an unbelievable effort to undress.'

In that cell, she asked Pauline, 'When we're misunderstood and judged unfavorably, what good does it do to defend or explain ourselves?' Thérèse wasn't merely unconcerned with mortal opinion; she was taking her leave of earth, greedy for every last opportunity to be misunderstood and humiliated, 'the means of remaining very little.'

In May, once Thérèse gave in and admitted to the prioress that she was too weak to carry on with her regular duties, Marie de Gonzague consulted with doctors and ordered a succession of treatments that, while useless against the disease, did provide further mortification. As the vesicatories hadn't relieved the coughing that made it impossible for her to sleep, Thérèse now submitted to *points de feu,* or the application of burning needles, to the flesh on her back, again to stimulate circulation and healing. During this process she leaned against a table, dwelling on the suffering of the martyrs, while the doctors and the prioress 'kept up a sprightly conversation of banalities.'

'Persecution has changed in form,' Thérèse wrote Père Roulland, adding that 'all missionaries are martyrs by desire and will.' She spoke of his trials in China, but her own were more immediate. With the warmer weather, she was ordered to walk each day in the garden – comparing herself to the 'poor wandering Jew' – and on days when the doctor did not apply the cautery needle, Céline was forced to do it instead.

In response to a request from Mother Henriette, a Parisian Carmelite who was ill and to whom Mother Marie had spoken of Thérèse's poetry and her holiness, Thérèse wrote 'An Unpetalled Rose,' celebrating total sacrifice and abandonment to Christ. It had been, in previous years, Thérèse's pleasure to take the novices into the cloister's courtyard and strew rose petals under the crucifix. 'The rose in its splendor,' intact, was not the rose she wanted to be; she chose to spend herself entirely, to be 'unpetalled . . . flung out / To blow away . . . To be no more.' Christ was the 'beauty Supreme' for which she 'must die.'

Mother Henriette liked the poem, with one reservation. She found its vision of sacrifice incomplete and wrote back requesting another stanza in which, after death, God gathered up the scattered petals and reassembled the flower so that it might shine for eternity. Thérèse refused: that wasn't what she'd meant at all. She wanted annihilation, 'to be unpetalled forever, to make God happy. Period.'

The drive toward nothingness was hard for Thérèse's less mystical Catholic sisters to understand. Their lives as religious were dedicated to a kind of account book of sacrifices made in order to purchase spiritual advancement. Thérèse's impulse to destroy self seemed to them a repudiation of orthodoxy, of the idea of individual salvation and resurrection, the reward promised to the virtuous.

'Die now,' Pauline wrote, crying so that she could hardly see the page, unable to sever mortal bonds with the ruthlessness of her little sister. 'Die quickly so that my heart may no longer have any attachment here below.' Incredibly, it was not until the end of May 1897 that she learned of Thérèse's previous, initial period of hemorrhaging, now more than a year past. Abashed by her older sister's shock, Thérèse asked Pauline's pardon, using a metaphor to which she would return. If she had hidden something of the body's 'envelope' from her little mother, Pauline may be sure that 'the letter' – her soul – 'is yours.'

Very little strength was left within her sister, and Pauline thought carefully before asking Marie de Gonzague to order Thérèse to continue her autobiographical work. She didn't want to further exhaust Thérèse, but, convinced of the value of the work, she found herself unable to resist any means of draining what wisdom and grace she could from a young woman who she believed had direct access to God. Letters from Pauline to Thérèse – letters written in private, even as she was spending evenings with their recipient – made one plea after another for Thérèse's prayers and posthumous attentions, wringing holy metaphors from every possible source. 'This evening,' Pauline confessed in one such note, 'near the Blessed Virgin there was a very bright candle that had overflowed and the wax formed, on the side, the veritable mold of a little lamb pleading. I thought that the light was you and the little lamb was myself.'

During the first week of June, Thérèse embarked on the final portion of what would become her *Story of a Soul*. She wrote sitting in the garden, in the invalid chair that her father had used and which the Guérins delivered to the convent so that she might enjoy a little time outdoors. Under the shade of chestnut trees, she was not 'able to write ten lines without being disturbed'; one or another member of the community interrupted her with 'idle chatter,' with cut flowers she would 'prefer to see swaying on their stems,' tokens of affection she had perhaps taught herself to undervalue.

In her moments of solitude, she recounted a story to provide an example of how she had grown in her ability to shrug off human judgment. Interestingly, it is a story of a key, and not any key but that to the communion grate, the same that unlocks the Body of Christ, offering mystical union to every Catholic. In July of 1891, recently appointed as aide to the sacristan, Thérèse had this key in her possession and came to return it to Marie de Gonzague while the prioress was ill with bronchitis. Met at the door by another sister, she was prevented from seeing Mother Marie, from interrupting her rest. But Thérèse insisted: it was her 'duty' to return the key, and she 'wanted absolutely to enter in spite of the fact that she was pushing the door to prevent me.' Of course, the argument woke the prioress and Thérèse fled, allowing the other nun to accuse her of being 'disagreeable.'

'My heart was beating so rapidly that it was impossible for me to go far,' she remembered of the event, and yet she sat on the stairs not to get her breath but to savor a 'victory' she'd won over herself, the victory of allowing another sister to misinterpret her, of not remaining to vindicate her position.

Like many of Thérèse's stories, the story of the key is one of minutiae, 'of making so much fuss over such little things.' And yet small events form most of the fabric of a life, and the memory presents a drama replete with iconic figures: the mother, ill and unavailable in her cell; the daughter with a key to return – *the key* to everlasting life; the guard at the door who introduces a misunderstanding; the failure to reach the powerful mother; the flight into lonely 'victory.' Six years later, Thérèse was still sifting through these highly charged moments, savoring a lesson: the failure to connect was all to the good if it taught her to despise human measures. What wouldn't she have construed as purifying?

Thérèse had arrived at a point far beyond her old struggle

with scruples, one she described to her cousin Marie of the Eucharist as 'a lot of self-seeking, your griefs, your sorrows, all that is centered on yourself, like spinning around on the same pivot.' The difference between the vicious circle of narcissism cloaked as piety and the amusing top spun by Jesus would be the force behind the revolutions. Was it the whip of self-seeking or the hand of God? Before she died, would Thérèse herself reach perfect detachment, become that mystical bride lost in Love? Certainly her hunger had been so long thwarted, and was now so great, that she considered only eternal satisfactions. 'Nothing that is called happiness in the world can satisfy it,' she wrote her sisters, speaking of her heart. 'I find nothing on earth that makes me happy.'

'Detach your heart from the worries of this earth, and above all from creatures,' she exhorted Sister Martha of Jesus.

'Work solely for Him and do nothing for self or for creatures,' she advised Abbé Bellière.

Struggling for breath as she wrote in her wheelchair parked in the shade, Thérèse still fantasized about a foreign mission. What attracted her, she admitted to Mother Marie, was not so much the occasion to proselytize and win converts, but 'I dream of a monastery where I shall be unknown, where I would suffer from poverty, the lack of affection, and finally, the exile of the heart.'

Abandonment to divine love was the only means Thérèse had found of defending herself from human abandonment – by mother, father, sisters, the thoughtless girls at convent school. Mysticism offered her a means of redefining the experience that had proved again and again so devastating. To reduce it to the logic of the playground, if she couldn't beat them, she'd join them: Thérèse would forsake Thérèse. Abandonment would no longer be the enemy, but the goal, whose victim remained the same: earthly Thérèse, vulnerable Thérèse, human Thérèse.

The flow of language, like blood from a wound, testifies to the violence of the experience. Thérèse consistently evoked the idea of immersion in divine love with verbs that were destructive, murderous, vengeful. To achieve union with the divine, self must be *humiliated,* it must be *exiled, broken, burned, despised, unpetalled, pierced, incinerated, rent, consumed, flooded, flung out, squandered, withered* ... There were many ways to evoke the rage of the forsaken child.

If anger was unavoidable, so, for Thérèse, was its object. Whom could she destroy? Not her mother, pious in life, saintly in death, 'Princess and Lady of Honor of the Heavenly Court'; not her four virginal sisters, praying in convents; and certainly not her grieving, self-sacrificing father. Only herself, the problem child whose problem was self and whom the wisdom of the Church gave Thérèse the most praiseworthy reasons to destroy: Love. The saving of souls. The consolation of Christ.

Nothing could be more arduous than the methodical dismemberment of desire, the renunciation of pleasure, the brutal suppression of personality, but the reward was incalculable: the clamor of self silenced, its ravenous hunger satisfied once and for all; the threat of separation undone; suffering which, Thérèse rightly judged, had been plentiful in her short life, vanquished. Christ, whose love she characterized as wine, dangled a narcotic promise, even as she endured a torture that most consumptives offset with morphine.

Yet, for a girl wedded to the obliteration of self, heaven was entirely personal, cast in the shape of her parents. 'If you find me dead one morning, don't be troubled,' she told Pauline, 'it's because Papa, God, will have come to get me.' This is no turn of phrase, as another comment from the same period demonstrates. Anticipating her reception into heaven, Thérèse worried that her expectations of its wonder and perfection might in fact be dashed by a less amazing reality. 'So I'm already thinking that if I'm not surprised enough, I will pretend to be surprised just to please God. There isn't any danger that I'll allow Him to see my disappointment.' The echo of her Christmas conversion is so strong, it seems impossible that it might be unconscious, but one of Thérèse's most compelling and curious qualities is this seemingly impossible conflation of mystical reach and infantile wish.

'Ah the Lord is so good to me that it is quite impossible for me to fear Him. He has always given me what I desire, *or rather* He has made me desire what He wants to give me' (emphasis added). A skeptic would say that Thérèse gave the name *God* to her internal strategy for survival. But perhaps every mystic finds the way to the divine through a rent in his or her psyche, a wound that might, in a lesser soul, result in self-absorption, vanity, avarice, envy.

IN 1927, thirty years after the death of Thérèse Martin, nearly a half-century after the discovery of the bacillus that caused tuberculosis, Thomas Mann attempted to demystify consumption, using impressions gathered in 1912 from a sanatorium in Davos, Switzerland, where his wife had been a patient. But the characters of *The Magic Mountain* obeyed a will greater than their author's; they perpetuated what not only Thérèse, and not only Catholics, wanted to believe. Mann's antihero, Hans Castorp, ascended to this rarefied disease, joining an exclusive community of consumptives. Against a celestial backdrop, he succumbed to the spell of a woman who moved 'almost without sound,' and that woman, Clavdia Chauchat, gave Hans what he considered 'his treasure,' an 'X-ray portrait showing not her face but the delicate bony structure of the upper half of her body, the organs of the thoracic cavity, surrounded by the pale, ghostlike envelope of flesh.'

Luminous, radiant, seductive, a tracing of light on emulsion: 'How often had he looked at it, how often pressed it to his lips.'

Tubercle bacilli attack all organs, but tuberculosis is understood as an ailment – a transformation – of the chest, the locus of the soul. Of respiration, inspiration, expiration. The disease itself, as Susan Sontag observed, is granted qualities of the 'upper, spiritualized body'; and even before X-rays rendered the tubercular literally transparent, exposing their lungs and hearts to view, the wasting of patients was described in terms of transparency. This convention existed in the United States as well as in Europe. In *Little Women*, Louisa May Alcott eulogized her sister Lizzie in the character of the consumptive Beth, whose face had 'a strange transparent look about it, as if the mortal was being slowly refined away, and the immortal shining through the frail flesh with an indescribably pathetic beauty.'

Countless novels, plays, and paintings underscored the popular and comforting conceit that the tubercular patient was released from the body, made incorporeal, that consumption was a heightened rather than a lowered state, a process of illumination, in effect: flesh burned to create light. In truth, one is freed only from a healthy body; illness makes its own demands and clamor.

By July, Thérèse had written her last poem and was forced to abandon work on her autobiography, the last sentence a penciled fragment ending with the word *love*. Her story was now in the hands of her note-taking sisters and cousin, women who would be called upon by the Vatican to share their impressions of an obscure young nun dying in the Carmel of Lisieux, one for whom the cloister wall provided no immunity from the sentimentalization of disease.

Thérèse's hemorrhages began again on July 6 and continued intermittently for twenty-nine days, bleeding so severe that it seemed to those who cared for her that she was coughing up fragments of tissue – like 'bits of liver,' her cousin Marie of the Eucharist reported, adding, 'She'll cough up a generous glassful in a quarter of an hour.'

Liquefaction: Thérèse's body was disappearing, growing thinner and thinner, as she became the essence, the vehicle, of redemption. Long ago, following her Christmas conversion, Thérèse had determined to take her place at the foot of the cross, to receive the blood of salvation and in turn pour it out for the forgiveness of sins. It is in the context of such a desire that we understand her exultation over a death that was by any measure grotesque.

'She had coughed up blood during the night,' Céline wrote in her notebook. 'Very joyful, with her childish gestures, she was showing me the saucer from time to time. Often she pointed to its rim with a sad little look that meant "I would have liked it to be up to there!"'

Thérèse lay in her cell. Only by means of complete immobilization and ice packs was the hemorrhaging controlled. On July 8, too weak to stand, she was carried downstairs to the infirmary and placed in the same bed in which Mother Geneviève had died almost six years before. From a window she could look out on the cloister garden, the crucifix for which she had unpetalled her roses. The statue of the Virgin of the Smile was carried downstairs from the niche outside her cell and placed where she could see it. Pinned to her bed's brown privacy curtain were pictures of the Virgin and of the martyr Théophane Vénard, as well as those of Thérèse's dead brothers and sisters. Using a pen – dipping it into an inkwell – was impossible while lying flat; when her strength permitted, Thérèse used a pencil to write to her sisters within the cloister, to Léonie outside, to her aunt and uncle Guérin, and to her two missionary brothers – eighteen letters in all, 'victories of love over her physical exhaustion,' as her translator, John Clarke, O.C.D., noted. While earlier correspondence never mentioned her illness, these last letters speak almost exclusively of approaching death: Thérèse insisted on her happiness in suffering for as long as God willed it, and she fantasized about the life to come, about all she would do after her death – empowered by death – for those she loved. Soon, an angel would be their advocate. 'Your joy will be greater still when, instead of reading a few lines written with a trembling hand, you will feel my soul near your own. Ah! I am certain God will allow me to pour out His favors lavishly.'

'You are drawing the tears from our eyes when we see you so joyful in the midst of suffering,' her aunt Céline responded on July 20. 'When I think of you, a flower so pure and so chaste, I begin to despise humanity,' Uncle Isidore continued in the same vein, on the 24th. 'You do not even suspect the frightful and hideous depth of the wounds gnawing away at humanity.' Each letter she received celebrated her purity, her piety; each of her correspondents took Thérèse at her word when she spoke of the joy of suffering. Who among them might have suspected what she admitted to Pauline, that when she looked out of her window and saw a black shadow under the chestnut trees, she found her soul 'in a similar hole'?

On the table by her bed was a glass filled with a foul-tasting medicine that looked red and inviting. A visitor pointed to what she assumed was a tasty cordial and made an envious comment. 'This is what happens,' Thérèse remarked to Pauline. 'It has always seemed to them that I was drinking exquisite liqueurs, and it was bitterness. But no,' she qualified immediately, 'my life hasn't been bitter because I know how to turn all bitterness into something joyful and sweet.'

Able to sit up for only two hours each day, when she could hold a book Thérèse read from the Gospels, from Thomas à Kempis's *Imitation of Christ,* from the works of John of the

Cross. When she had the breath to speak, she said a few words to her sisters. Pauline, who was reading carefully through her memoirs, asked questions to clarify certain passages of the book she would eventually edit.

In an attempt to feed Thérèse something she could digest, the doctor prescribed a condensed milk diet, which she found repugnant and about which she made a few wry jokes, referring to herself as a 'milk baby,' alluding both to her little-ness and to milk's metaphorical significance: the love of God transmitted by the Virgin.

She had high fevers and drenching sweats; she felt she was suffocating. She coughed, she vomited, she bled. And yet, even as her cousin Marie of the Eucharist catalogued these miseries, she wrote that Thérèse 'always had to be saying something funny.' She couldn't help but try to offset her visi-tors' discomfort at witnessing so torturous an illness, and even elicited laughs from the doctor when he visited, some-times twice in a day.

Frustrated by the unpredictable course of an illness that left her always on the brink of death without actually deliver-ing her, Thérèse reminded her audience that she was resting on the very mattress on which Mother Geneviève had endured one crisis after another, receiving extreme unction three times while waiting for release. 'What an unfortunate bed,' Thérèse complained. 'When one is in it, one always misses the train.'

Among the positive images she used to evoke death – winning lottery tickets, cakes, sublime music – those of a tran-sition to the afterlife beginning at the train station recur most frequently during her last months and recall letters written by Zélie that described her youngest daughter's relationship to the Alençon terminal. 'I'm like a child at a railway station,' Thérèse told Pauline, 'waiting for her Papa and Mama to put her on a train; alas they don't come, and the train pulls out! However there are others, and I'll not miss all of them!'

And: 'I cough and I cough! I'm just like a locomotive when it arrives at the station: I'm arriving also at a station: heaven, and I'm announcing it.'

Thérèse had spent her whole life waiting for reunions. Even at one, she waited for the time she would see her mother. Two or three years old, she waited for her older sisters to come home from school, a paradise of company for the lonely child, afraid of separations. The train took her sisters away, and it returned them to her. 'She wanted absolutely to go into the waiting room to go and get Pauline . . . running ahead with a joy that was pleasing to see, but when she saw that we had to return without . . . Pauline, she cried all the way home,' Zélie wrote to her daughter Pauline at boarding school.

With Zélie, the two-year-old Thérèse was transported by train to her aunt Dosithée (the same who had predicted her sainthood) at the Visitation convent at Le Mans. There she had her first experience of a mother superior, who gave her gifts and blessings, and of a cloister grille that divided people and frightened her to tears, making her choke.

And, of course, it was a train that took Zélie to Lourdes and brought her home late. 'Your father was waiting for us for an hour,' Zélie wrote Pauline, 'with the two little ones.'

*

In preparation for her imminent journey, Thérèse attempted with the help of Pauline to recall 'the sins she could have committed through the senses' in order to confess them before receiving the last rites. Her abstemiousness had been so complete as an adult that she was forced to rake through childhood memories for a transgression, settling on the sense of smell: 'I remember during my last trip from Alençon to Lisieux' – this would have been at the age of fourteen – 'I used a bottle of eau de cologne . . . and I did this with pleasure.'

Without distractions – without writing, without instructing the novices or sewing the linens, without reading, without sweeping or washing – Thérèse was left alone with her flesh, the body in which she had 'never been at ease.' When a sister picked a violet for Thérèse in the garden, Pauline recorded this in her yellow notebook:

Our little Thérèse said to me, looking at the flower:
'Ah! the scent of violets!'
Then she made a sign to me to know if she could smell it without failing in mortification.

Sent some fruit that she was unable to eat, Thérèse held and examined each piece. 'I get so much pleasure out of touching fruit, especially peaches, and I like to see them near me,' she told Pauline, and was immediately stricken by the admission of sensuality. 'Perhaps that's not good?'

Just as Thérèse was tormented by private fears of mortality, so did she remain afraid of corruption, and her fears expressed themselves in an obsessive focus on the body – the stubborn and demanding body that was supposed to have disappeared. Until the end, she had to remain vigilant. Even a pleasure so small as that taken in the scent of a flower or the down of a peach might represent a fault line, a minute crack through which the devil might enter or salvation seep away.

On July 30, the hemorrhaging continued without cease; Thérèse felt she was suffocating. Doctor de Cornière prescribed ether to help her breathe, and Canon Maupas came to anoint her. The community assumed that she couldn't last the night, and, in the room next to the infirmary, sacristans set out what was needed to ready a Carmelite for burial: candles, holy water, and her *paillasse* (straw mattress), carried down from her cell. Thérèse noted their preparations with pleasure. Still joking to relieve the oppression of a death-watch, 'Put the candle in my hand,' she asked between gasping breaths. 'But not the candlestick, it's too ugly.'

It would seem that Thérèse, used as she was to a stark and punishing internal landscape, couldn't bear to be surrounded by tear-stained faces, perhaps because the grief of her sisters quickened her own.

ABRUPTLY, on August 5, the hemorrhages stopped, and Thérèse's condition stabilized, although she remained so short of breath that she was often unable to speak. On August 6, Doctor de Cornière went on vacation, leaving prescriptions, and the Guérins, having consulted with the doctor, left town for Vichy, where Uncle Isidore was seeking a cure for his gout.

Excused from singing Matins, Pauline came to the infirmary each morning before breakfast to visit Thérèse. She plied her sister with questions and probed for slight spiritual realignments, determined to harvest every nuance of the unfolding apotheosis. One day, as evening approached, she lamented that Thérèse had said nothing for posterity that day. 'Today, I'll have nothing to write,' she recorded, unashamed of what strikes readers as a kind of torture.

Notes and correspondence reveal that not just the Martin sisters but the entire community speculated feverishly about which feast day Thérèse might expire on. When the Transfiguration of Our Lord came and went on August 6, the would-be mourners/celebrants settled on the next suitably auspicious and significant occasion – August 15, the Assumption of Our Lady. A deathwatch offered excitement and entertainment, release from the oppressively repetitive routine as well as a chance to witness the moving hand of God. Clearly, Thérèse tired of the scrutiny. 'Don't talk of a date,' she begged, but it was too late to argue for peace or privacy. Her death had become a shared work in progress, an agonizingly slow drama involving the whole convent.

'What shall you die of?' one of the sisters is said to have asked. (As the disease had introduced more than one life-threatening complication, her question would not have been as senseless as it seems.)

'I'm dying from death!' Thérèse answered with uncharacteristic tartness.

On Sunday, August 15, she developed sharp pains in her left side, and her legs began to swell. In Doctor de Cornière's absence, her cousin Jeanne's husband, Doctor la Neele, was given permission by Marie de Gonzague to enter the cloistered infirmary. Examining Thérèse, he found her right lung 'completely lost, filled with tubercles in the process of softening,' and the lower left lobe affected as well – it was this that was causing the stabbing sensation in her side. By now Thérèse was getting so little oxygen that she had to pause after each word to breathe. Marie of the Eucharist wrote her father, Isidore Guérin, that the 'tuberculosis has reached its final stage,' hardly a surprising report but significant in that the diagnosis made by Doctor la Neele was the first to include the word *tuberculosis*. Like cancer, or AIDS, or any undefeated killer, the name itself was taboo, avoided even by members of the medical profession.

Too weak to endure the long ceremonial required of communicants, Thérèse received the Eucharist for the last time on Thursday, August 19, and she felt the subsequent deprivation keenly, sobbing until she choked and considering it a punishment even more severe than the pain that was driving her past the point of reason. In the wake of the tuberculosis attacking her intestines came gangrene. Pauline's yellow notebook recorded that Thérèse vomited almost continually from that point on. 'Her stomach was hard as a rock. She was no longer able to perform bodily functions except with terrible pains.' Subjected to the indignity of enemas, which must have provided intense humiliation to a woman ashamed of even a healthy body, she found no relief. 'It's as though I were on fire inside,' Thérèse said.

Céline, the assistant infirmarian, slept in an adjoining cell, and she came to her sister whenever she cried out, but what comfort could she offer? If she propped her up to ease the suffocation, Thérèse felt as if she were sitting on spikes. She was emaciated, covered with bedsores; her bones came literally through her skin.

'*Je souffre,*' she said over and over. I suffer. And each time she insisted that Céline answer: '*Tant mieux.*' All the better. The responsorial was a way of stitching each moment to the passion of Christ, to his side that was pierced, to his thirst that was unquenchable, to the suffocating agony that ends a crucifixion.

'She was never attacked outwardly by the devil,' Céline testified at the beatification process, but one morning Céline woke to 'find her in great distress, there seemed to be some kind of painful struggle going on.' Thérèse told her sister that 'something very strange happened last night. God asked me to suffer for you, and I agreed. My pain was immediately doubled.' She felt the devil holding her in an iron grip, she felt his rage, and she knew he wanted to prevent her from getting the slightest relief in order that she succumb to despair.

After Thérèse's death, some would judge that the devil had found a willing colleague in the prioress. Opiates were 'almost universally used' to alleviate the pain and anguish of tuberculosis, and by now what little breath Thérèse had was spent on whimpering and crying out, an agony awful to witness. Upon his return, Doctor de Cornière advised injections of morphine. Mother Marie refused. Holiness was Carmel's stock-in-trade, and nothing could induce her to compromise the 'good death' to which her potential saint aspired. As Thérèse herself gasped, 'I'm suffering very much, but am I suffering very well? That's the point!'

The mandate to transcend was now public, subjected to the scrutiny of those beyond the community, doctors and extended family, the eager rumor mill of a provincial Catholic town, but even the faithful could be weakened by torture. Infirmarians must be careful to keep all medication out of a patient's reach, Thérèse cautioned Céline. Tempted to take her own life, had she been an atheist she would not have hesitated, not even for the space of a second, she said.

In a similar vein of wishing to spare others the mortifications she jealously guarded, Thérèse made further recommendations for the care of the sick: more heat, better food, softer sheets. After her death, too late for her to enjoy them, these improvements were made.

On the afternoon of Friday, August 27, her pain suddenly eased, only to be followed by a symptom more troubling: 'She was unexpectedly assailed by a real temptation to gluttony. All sorts of exotic dishes flashed through her imagination, and she was obsessed with desire for them.' This recollection from Pauline during the beatification process seems harsh in its interpretation and is perhaps better understood as an attempt to manufacture a last morality play out of what was normal physiological process. Starvation inevitably inspires fantasies of food, and Thérèse was starving. Astonished and embarrassed by the force of her hunger and by her ability for a few days to eat without vomiting, she welcomed all the Guérins provided: soups and meat, chicken, artichokes, even an infamous chocolate éclair, a pastry she requested and whose potential to corrupt was overstated, to say the least. But if sin could arrive in the form of a pleasing smell, how much greater was the transgression associated with food, food that had substance, taste as well as aroma, food that 'sustains the body, corrupt life on earth, and thereby kills the soul, life everlasting.'

'I have an appetite that's making up for my whole life,' Thérèse lamented. 'I always ate like a martyr, and now I could devour everything. It seems to me I'm dying of hunger.'

A photograph taken on August 30 – the last of the living Thérèse – recorded her final trip outdoors. Rolled in her bed onto the cloister walk, just outside the door to the choir, she holds her crucifix in her right hand, rose petals in her left. Her face has at last lost its characteristic roundness and betrays nothing so much as exhaustion; her eyes meet ours with the slow, affectless stare of someone for whom a smile or a frown costs too great an effort. Not merely wasted, she is small within the photograph's composition: Céline has included a corner of the garden and framed the bed within one of the walkway's arches. From out of its deep, black shadow, bed linens, nightdress, and rumpled veil glow white.

Thérèse's final remission and excursion through corporeal pleasure were finished on September 14, and her last days were characterized by a weakness so extreme that the slightest noise upset her; the ministering touch of one of her sisters was an assault on her nerves. Still, she answered questions; she never failed in patience. 'Both Sister Marie of the Sacred Heart and I took her pulse for a long period of time,' Pauline recorded. 'She didn't show any sign of fatigue at first in order not to cause us anguish, but finally, not being able to stand any more pain, she began to cry.'

But, 'You don't have any intuition about the day of your death?' Pauline pressed.

And, 'Who will receive your last look?' everyone wanted to know. Like the loyal child she was, Thérèse answered that were God to leave her gaze free, the good-bye was promised to the prioress.

Outside the infirmary window, a dead leaf hung from a strand of spider's silk, and Thérèse watched as it twisted in the breeze, 'a picture of myself,' she called it, 'my life hangs only on a light thread.' And yet hang it did, for fifteen days.

On Wednesday, September 29, a 'very heavy' death rattle began and, even without talking, Thérèse gasped for air. The community assembled around her bed to recite the Latin prayers for the dying.

'Mother, is this the agony? What must I do to die?' she beseeched Mother Marie, who could tell her only that the doctor confirmed that death was imminent.

That evening, Abbé Faucon came and heard her last confession, proclaiming her soul 'confirmed in grace.' Given a teaspoon of morphine syrup, she begged to be left alone during the night, but the prioress insisted that Céline and Marie keep watch, with Pauline in the adjoining room. They slept, while Thérèse remained awake, holding a glass of water so as not to have to ask for any.

'I no longer believe in death for me,' she said the following day, only hours from release. 'I believe only in suffering.'

'You never seem to be tired of suffering,' Pauline had remarked a few days earlier. 'Are you tired of it?'

'No! When I can't take it anymore, I can't take it, and that's it!'

On September 30, for the first time in weeks, Thérèse sat up without assistance and called on the Virgin to come to her aid, imploring God to take pity on her.

'All of a sudden,' at five o'clock, her face changed and Pauline 'understood it was her last agony.' The community assembled as they had the previous day, all twenty-four nuns crowding into the infirmary, welcomed with a smile from Thérèse. They watched and listened as a 'terrible rattle tore her chest,' saw that her face was blue, her hands purple. It was at last, as Thérèse said it would be, the occasion of her arrival into her true life, and the work of her dying was like that of childbirth: her limbs shook, and she soaked her covers and mattress with sweat. The community watched for two hours until, at seven, Mother Marie dismissed them.

'Am I not going to die?' Thérèse begged when she found herself alone once more with her family, her sisters and her mother superior.

'Yes, my poor little one,' Mother Marie answered. 'But God perhaps wills to prolong it.'

'All right, all right, I would not want to suffer for a shorter time.'

She looked at the crucifix in her hand. 'Oh, I love Him,' she gasped. 'My God I love you.'

Transported by ecstasy, her face went from its mottled dark hue to white, her eyes brilliant with peace and with joy. The prioress called all the community back to witness how 'she made certain beautiful movements with her head, as though someone had divinely wounded her with an arrow of love, then had withdrawn the arrow to wound her again.' The arrival of the Heavenly Bridegroom, the paradoxically sexual and purifying Christ, like the father whose kisses ensured his daughters' virginity, was described in detail in the notes Thérèse's sisters took as they watched her die.

Pauline didn't measure the minutes but said her ecstasy lasted 'the space of a Credo,' as long, we are made to understand, as it might take Thérèse to recite the tenets of her faith, to reunite her with the long absent joy of faith.

At 7:20 on the evening of September 30, Thérèse Martin, age twenty-four years, died.

Outside the infirmary window, Pauline recorded in her notebook, the strand of silk that had held the dead leaf broke.

'After her death' – her consummation – 'she had a heavenly smile. She was ravishingly beautiful . . . she didn't seem any more than twelve or thirteen years old.'

Returned to a state of preadolescent innocence, that of a child bride, Thérèse's body was washed and dressed in her Carmelite habit, her black veil crowned with a white bridal wreath, her *paillasse* and pillow strewn with lilies.

Céline set up her camera to record a last image of her sister. Eyes closed, head inclined to the right, Thérèse looks more beautiful in death than ever she had in life. Her features seem to have been refined rather than ravaged or coarsened by suffering; they genuinely convey the sort of beatific peace we imagine saints to possess.

AT HER DEATH, Thérèse left three manuscripts: the first, dedicated to Pauline, was the 'family souvenir'; the second, written for Marie, concerned doctrine; the third, addressed to Mother Marie de Gonzague, supplied the prioress with information to use in her obituary notice. Mother Marie was willing for all three manuscripts to be published together as one work, with the understanding that the book be dedicated to her alone.

Pauline, by now an artist of compromise, agreed to this condition. She divided her sister's memoirs into ten chapters, imposing grammar and conventional spelling on what had been written hurriedly, subjected to the interruptions of work and illness. 'It is the means God will use to grant my desire,' Thérèse had told her sister on Sunday, July 11. She was sorry that she hadn't had the time to finish and refine her work, but she had what seems a premonition of its value; she knew there was 'something in it for all tastes.' Thérèse made Pauline the equivalent of her literary executrix and encouraged her sister to add and delete as she saw fit, as long as she preserved the essence of her 'little way.'

'Speak to no one about my manuscript before it is published,' she'd warned. 'If you act otherwise, the devil will lay more than one trap to hinder God's work, a very important work!'

'I am a cluster of red grapes,' Thérèse had written in one of her poems. Pauline made the grapes 'golden.' She sweetened and conventionalized what she found on the page, and when a passage struck her as overly intimate, she excised it. After Pauline's death in 1951, her changes were undone, but for as long as they lasted they made little difference. Thérèse had been correct in her judgment that there was something in the book for everyone, and what gaps she left in her story were quickly filled by the testimony of her sisters.

What did the life of Thérèse Martin offer? A map to heaven, most obviously, but the appeal of *Story of a Soul* was not limited to the moribund or the morbidly pious. Unconsciously, Thérèse provided a powerful anodyne for a number of immediate and worldly discomforts. The last decades of the nineteenth century had presented disconcerting advances to women in particular. Industrialization made for respectable employment outside the home (usually in garment factories); contraceptives dangled sexual liberation (from both childbearing and marriage); education closed the literacy gap between the genders (and ensured the success of serialized fiction); the suffrage movement offered political voice; increased social mobility and the 'wane of the romantic code' made room for the arrival of 'new' emancipated females, whose habits might include dancing, smoking, even drinking in public.

A ready-made audience beset by fin de siècle anxieties over the appropriate role of women seized upon Thérèse's romantic bourgeois vision. Here was the (reactionary) comfort of traditional, emblematic femininity. Eternally presexual and childlike, Thérèse had chosen a respectable means of power for women: invalidism. Dying of love, she never saw herself – nor was she perceived – as impotent but as divinely set apart. Her incarceration in a provincial convent made staying at home and caring for children seem comparatively expansive; her fear of the body as a collection of portals vulnerable to the devil validated nervousness over sexual freedom; her exaltation of confession and prayer made voting irrelevant; her many renunciations underscored the dangers of experience.

Thérèse's repetition of the word *white,* to choose an obvious example – and one whose littleness would appeal to its author – itself amounted to an antiphon of renunciation and rescue. White flower, white lily, white lamb, white dove, white snow, white bride: the woman without stain succumbed to what was popularly referred to as the White Death, which didn't so much kill as exalt her, at least in the eyes of the faithful, who didn't need to analyze their love for the Little Flower. She was their advocate, their means of approaching and appeasing God. They prayed to her, they prayed through her, and their prayers were answered.

During the last three months of her life, Thérèse had fantasized about the future. She would 'spend her heaven doing good on earth.' And every material thing she left behind, flowers she had touched as well as nail parings and fallen hairs, would be of use. 'Gather up these petals, little sisters, they will help you to perform favors later on. . . . Don't lose one of them,' she cautioned.

By September 6, 1910, when her body was exhumed from the Lisieux cemetery, what remained of it examined for supernatural surprises (there were none), Carmel was receiving as many as fifty letters a day giving testimony to miracles granted by Thérèse. Most of these would not have met the criteria demanded by the beatification cause, now under way, but this was of no concern to the people who believed in her power and whose numbers increased in a manner that confounded even her sisters, who had worked to create and commodify Thérèse. 'What a business to come down on us in our old age!' Pauline lamented to the Martins' cousin Jeanne la Neele. 'I could never have imagined even the smallest part of this conflagration when I timidly sent out the first spark.'

Story of a Soul guaranteed Carmel an industry that far outperformed all those modest means by which convents usually cobble together a subsistence – the making of hosts, the sewing of altar cloths and chasubles and scapulars, the painting of devotional images.

'From the start,' Céline testified in 1910, 'there were people looking for souvenirs of the servant of God. We have had to send them out in thousands. I am responsible for any objects that once belonged to Sister Thérèse, and I am amazed to see sheets, bed curtains, and articles of clothing already gone, though we cut them up into tiny fragments.' Even the slats of her bed and the floorboards of her cell were reduced to splinters and affixed to prayer cards bearing her image. 'From 1897 to 1925 the output reached the incredible figure of 30,500,000 pictures and 17,500,000 relics.' Incredible indeed – either her cell was atomized, or the fragments multiplied miraculously, as in the parable of the loaves and fishes. A publication, *Shower of Roses,* anthologized letters from her petitioners, reports of cures, and granted favors. From 1911 to 1926, they filled seven volumes, or thirty-two hundred pages.

When Thérèse's cause was before the Curia, beatification and canonization each required two certified miracles to ratify the Church's judgment of virtue. (Today, miracles are required for canonization only.) Usually – and ironically in this case, given Thérèse's hostility to the flesh, her mission to save souls even at the expense of the body – these were physical cures, healings that could not be explained by medical science. The mysterious odor of violets and roses that wafted down corridors, the unmistakable sense of Thérèse's presence in the sacristy: these may have convinced the sisters of Carmel that a saint was in their midst, but they were not the sort of manifestations acknowledged by the Church.

Neither did the ecclesiastical court use the testimony of any of the thousands of World War I soldiers who went into battle carrying a likeness or a medal of Thérèse, a sliver of her bed frame, and whose thanks for her rescue, engraved in marble, crowd the walls of the Carmel at Lisieux.

Instead, the Church settled on the cases of three of its own religious and one devout pilgrim. In 1906, a seminarist, Abbé Charles Anne of Lisieux, petitioned Thérèse for a cure for his pulmonary tuberculosis, which had reached its final stage. 'I did not come here to die; I came to work for God. You must heal me,' he prayed. He fell asleep and awoke completely restored to health, without fever, the cavity in his right lung vanished. In 1916, Thérèse appeared to Sister Louise of Saint Germaine and cured her of a life-threatening ulcer. In 1923, Sister Gabriella of Parma was cured of tuberculosis of the spine, and in the same year a Belgian girl, Marie Pellemans, whose pilgrimage to Lourdes had failed to relieve her tuberculosis, knelt at the tomb of Thérèse and was restored to health.

On March 26, 1923, Thérèse's remains were transported from a burial vault back to the Carmel at Lisieux by an ornate carriage drawn by four horses draped and plumed with white. An honor guard followed the ranks of bishops and cardinals; behind them marched a detachment of French and American soldiers. As a month remained before Thérèse's official beatification, the fifty thousand pilgrims who lined the streets of Lisieux were not allowed to sing or call out to the relics as they passed; the procession was accomplished in silence.

On May 18, 1945, Thérèse was canonized in Rome by Pope Pius XI, in the same church where, at fourteen years old, she had been pulled sobbing from the knees of Leo XIII. Five hundred thousand pilgrims crowded the basilica, which rang with their combined prayers.

A BRIDE'S WHITE SHOES.

A crown of white roses.

An hourglass.

A golden chalice.

A spade.

A lantern.

An inkwell.

Blond curls, abundantly long and thick, arranged to suggest the way her hair must have, once upon a time, fallen down her back and past her waist. Preserved under glass, they are close enough to touch – but for the glass – and convey the violence of scalping or headhunting, the more so in that the chamber of relics at the Lisieux Carmel is decorated in red. Thérèse's habit and her sandals, her writing desk, her crude implements and fine needlework – all are displayed against a backdrop the color of blood. Like everything in this drafty room with its dramatic lighting, the choice feels both inevitable and shocking.

Not only her hair, but each garment is displayed from the

back. Standing among them, more than a century after Thérèse's death, visitors cannot help but imagine the young woman turning around, looking over her shoulder to meet their eyes. As she does from every corner of her town of Lisieux: racks of postcards and shelves of books, posters, prayer cards, votive candles, coffee mugs, snow globes, paper knives, tea towels. Even an atheist would have to agree that Thérèse Martin had fulfilled her promise, come down from heaven to be among us.

In 1999, at the midpoint of an eight-year worldwide tour celebrating the centenary of her death, Thérèse's ornate reliquary drew crowds that amazed those who organized the posthumous foreign mission, part of the great work she had saved for her afterlife. In the United States, the three-hundred-pound wood and gilt casket under its domed Plexiglas shield passed through 106 cities and was greeted by 1.1 million people. At the National Shrine of the Little Flower, in Detroit's suburb of Royal Oak, fifty thousand people filed past during a sixteen-hour period on November 5. Twenty-five thousand who had waited outside the church in a freezing wind were turned away. At the end of each stop, the Plexiglas was clouded by handprints and by the impress of one upon another kiss.

From the United States to the Philippines, from the Philippines to Taiwan, from Taiwan to Hong Kong, from city to city and country to country, the bones of Thérèse Martin, once a child broken by loss, by abandonment, are borne into the future on a tide of love.

ACKNOWLEDGMENTS

Among the authors whose works are cited at the end of this volume, I am especially indebted to Guy Gaucher, O.C.D., and John Clarke, O.C.D., whose lucid chronologies and meticulous presentation of primary source material were invaluable.

For their support and guidance, I want to thank James Atlas, Carolyn Carlson, Barbara Flanagan, Janet Gibbs, Joan Gould, Colin Harrison, Gretchen E. Henderson, Adam Kirsch, Amanda Urban, and Lucia Watson.

NOTES

Abbreviations

SL Gaucher, Guy. *The Story of a Life: St. Thérèse of Lisieux.* New York: HarperCollins Publishers, 1987.

PT Gaucher, Guy. *The Passion of Thérèse of Lisieux.* New York: Crossroads Publishing, 1998.

ST O'Mahony, Christopher, ed. and trans. *St. Thérèse of Lisieux by Those Who Knew Her: Testimonies from the Process of Beatification.* Dublin: Veritas Publications, 1975.

SF Piat, Stéphane-Joseph, O.F.M. *The Story of a Family: The Home of St. Thérèse of Lisieux.* Rockford, Ill.: Tan Books and Publishers, 1948.

LC Thérèse de Lisieux, Saint. *St. Thérèse of Lisieux: Her Last Conversations.* Translated from the original manuscripts by John Clarke, O.C.D. Washington, D.C.: ICS Publications, 1977.

LT Thérèse de Lisieux, Saint. *Letters of Saint Thérèse of Lisieux.* Vols. I and II, *General Correspondence.* Translated from the original manuscripts by John Clarke, O.C.D. Washington, D.C.: ICS Publications, 1982, 1988.

PO Thérèse de Lisieux, Saint. *The Poetry of Saint Thérèse of Lisieux.* Translated by Donald Kinney, O.C.D. Washington, D.C.: ICS Publications, 1996.

SS Thérèse de Lisieux, Saint. *Story of a Soul: The Autobiography of St. Thérèse of Lisieux.* Translated from the original manuscripts by John Clarke, O.C.D. Washington, D.C.: ICS Publications, 1996.

1 'would never have suspected her sanctity': SL, 207.

1 'voice of the people': "We must lose no time in crowning the little saint with glory, if we do not want the voice of the people to anticipate us,' declared Cardinal Vico, Prefect of the Congregation of Rites.' Ibid., 210.

1 *Poor grain of sand . . . too glorious:* LT, 580, 612.

2 of whom three are women: The other two female Doctors of the Church are Saint Catherine of Siena and Saint Teresa of Ávila.

2 'God deigned to grant': SS, 15.

4 'story of a "steel bar"': 'the willpower, courage and resolution which it revealed made it seem to me the story of a steel bar.' Albino Luciani [later Pope John Paul I], *St. Thérèse of Lisieux: From Lisieux to the Four Corners of the World* (Strasbourg: Éditions du Signe, 1995), 23.

5 'let him deny himself': Matt. 16:24.

5 'bury their own dead': Luke 9:60.

5 'to the service of God': SS, 73.

6 'glance on the past': Ibid., 15.

6 'sad as a shroud': Letter to her brother, Isidore Guérin, November 7, 1865, SL, 9.

7 'See to the making of *Point d'Alençon*': SF, 33.

7 'whom I have prepared for you': Ibid., 40.

10 'slaves to fashion': Letter to Pauline, dated January 30, 1876, LT, 1221.

11 'are reunited up above': Ibid., 1205.

11 'I was born to have them': Letter to Céline Guérin, December 15, 1872, ibid., 1199.

12 'crown upon all my misfortunes': Letter to Isidore Guérin, December 23, 1866, SF, 114.

12 'glandular swelling': Letter to Isidore Guérin, April 23, 1865, ibid., 72.

13 'would have crossed a forest alone': Letter to Céline Guérin, January 13, 1867, ibid., 76.

13 'They were not lost forever': Letter to Céline Guérin, October 17, 1871, ibid., 98.

13 'arms so stiff and face so cold!': Letter to Isidore Guérin, June 27, 1865, ibid., 74.

14 'she sang with me': Letter to Céline Guérin, January 16, 1873, LT, 1200.

15 'Everyone tells me she is beautiful': Ibid.

15 'could no longer doubt it yesterday': Ibid.

15 'as all wet-nurses today are': Letter to Céline Guérin, December 15, 1872, ibid., 1199.

15 'this is her entire nourishment': Letter to Céline Guérin, January 16, 1873, ibid., 1200.

16 'very gay, very darling': Letter to Céline Guérin, December 13, 1873, ibid., 1209.

17 'story of this so-happy couple': Letter to Isidore Guérin, March 1864, SF, 61.

17 'until someone brings her back to me': Letter to Pauline, June 25, 1874, LT, 1211.

18 'So many steps, so many Mamma's!': Letter to Pauline, November 21, 1875, ibid., 1218.

18 'we must die to go there': Letter to Pauline, December 5, 1875, ibid., 1219.

18 'full of life': SS, 34.

18 'if she accuses herself': Letter to Pauline, May 21, 1876, LT, 1224–25.

19 'believing that all is lost': Letter to Pauline, December 5, 1875, ibid., 1219.

20 'never leaves her for one minute': Letter to Pauline, March 4, 1877, ibid., 1232.

21 'rather sleep there than say "yes"': Letter to Pauline, May 14, 1876, LT, 1223.

21 'a summary of my whole life': SS, 27.

21 'strange whistling in her chest': Letter to Céline Guérin, November 12, 1876, LT, 1227.

21 'experienced this more than once': Letter to Marie-Louise Morel, December 27, 1875, ibid., 1219.

22 'five times as much': Gen. 43:34.

22 'for her day and night': Letter to Céline Guérin, November 12, 1876, LT, 1227.

22 'invincible stubbornness': Letter to Pauline, May 14, 1876, ibid., 1223.

23 'to do whatever He wills!': Letter to Pauline, May 10, 1877, ibid., 1234.

23 'in the arms of her mother': Letter to Pauline, October 29, 1876, ibid., 1226.

25 'I am like all the rest': Letter to Céline Guérin, April 12, 1877, SF, 242.

25 'twinges returned as usual': Ibid., 244.

25 'model of insubordination': Letter to Pauline, March 12, 1877, ibid., 238.

26 'obeyed only the maid': Ibid.

26 'Léonie sobbed': Letter to Céline Guérin, June 14, 1877, ibid., 229.

27 'make her obey': Letter to Pauline, March 22, 1877, ibid., 240.

27 'as though completely crushed': Letter to Céline Guérin, December 17, 1876, ibid., 230.

28 'second mother in their aunt': Isidore Guérin quoted ibid., 248.

28 'from the armchair to bed': Ibid., 256.

28 'in times of peace and joy': Ibid.

28 'two poor little *exiles*': SS, 33. Emphasis added.

29 'looked and listened in silence': Ibid.

30 'It appeared large and dismal': Ibid., 34.

30 'Pauline will be Mama!': Ibid.

30 'sensitive to an excessive degree': Ibid.

31 'path that ran steeply uphill': SF, 264.

32 'might be an occasion of temptation': ST, 85.

32 'with a truly maternal love': SS, 35.

32 'read without help was 'heaven'': Ibid., 36.

33 'she asked permission for everything': ST, 23.

33 'nothing to envy in the first': SS, 45.

33 'sensitive to other people's sufferings': ST, 49.

34 'Earth again seemed a sad place': SS, 37.

34 'arranged according to my taste': Ibid., 39.

35   'poured out tears of repentance': Ibid.

36   'incomparable favor': Ibid., 44.

36   'caused me to admire him': Ibid., 49.

36   'filled the soul with profound thoughts': Ibid., 43.

37   'alone at the window of an attic': Ibid., 45.

37   'covered with a sort of apron': Ibid., 46.

37   'engraved so deeply': Ibid.

37   'I'll die with him!': Ibid., 48.

38   'loved him with all her heart': SL, 38.

38   'one of the most beautiful of my life': SS, 57.

39   'narrow and flighty': Ibid., 82.

39   'only bitterness in earth's friendships': Ibid., 83.

40   'saddest in my life': Ibid., 53.

40   'quiet, calm and reserved . . . dreamy': SL, 41.

41   'buried in my heart': SS, 58.

41   'faraway desert place': Ibid., 57.

41   'Thérèse had taken it seriously': Ibid., 57–58.

42   'better than become a nun': Ralph Gibson, *A Social History of French Catholicism, 1789–1914* (London: Routledge, 1989), 118.

43   'shining with such brightness': SS, 59.

43–44   'FAR from being mature': Ibid.

45   'touched me profoundly and made me cry': Ibid., 60.

45   'hallucinations several times a day': ST, 184.

45   'very serious': SS, 61.

46   'impossible to describe': ST, 86.

46   'for one single instant': SS, 62.

47   'had become ill on purpose': Ibid.

47   'remove it from my mind': Ibid., 64.

48   '"They want to poison me!"': Testimony of Marie Martin, ST, 87.

48   'She is here by my side': SS, 64n.

48   'lasted four or five minutes': ST, 87.

49   'ineffable benevolence and tenderness': SS, 65.

49   'happiness would then disappear': Ibid., 66.

50 'as if she had been my mother': John J. Delaney, ed., *A Woman Clothed with the Sun: Eight Great Apparitions of Our Lady* (New York: Image Books, 1961), 122.

50 'spiritual trial for the next four years': SS, 66.

50 'a feeling of profound horror': Ibid., 67.

51 'kisses her dear little daughter': Letter dated October 14, 1883 or 1884, LT, 177.

52 'first entrance into the world': SS, 73.

52 'to the service of God': Ibid.

52 'didn't think about death enough': Ibid.

53 'For you, I must die': PO, 204.

53–54 '2,773 acts of love or aspirations': ST, 24.

54 'already instructing [her] in secret': SS, 75.

54 'laughed heartily at me': Ibid., 74.

54 'eyes bright with joy': Ibid., 75.

54 'like few other children on earth': Ibid.

55 'made a spectacle': Ibid., 76.

55 'I give myself to you forever': Ibid.

55 'copious tears': SL, 52.

55 'did not satisfy [her] heart': SS, 79.

55–56 'without my understanding them very well': Ibid.

56 'our little feathered friends': Ibid., 81.

56 'especially Joan of Arc': Ibid., 72.

56 'terrible sickness of scruples': Ibid., 84.

57 'especially her teachers': Ibid., 85.

57 'while telling all my scruples': Ibid.

58 'so-called sins': ST, 88.

58 'as if she were dead': SS, 88.

58 'arranged to suit [her] taste': Ibid., 90.

58 'the portrait of Pauline': Ibid.

59 'cured for life': Ibid.

59 'lost its attraction': Ibid., 91.

59 'made a big fuss over everything': Ibid.

60 'had a weak character': Ibid.

60 'frequently moist with tears': Ibid., 92.

61 'night which sheds such light': Ibid., 97.

61 'this will be the last year!': Ibid., 98.

61 'pierced my heart': Ibid.

62 'being rocked for a long time': PO, 97.

62 'the treasure / Of virginity': Ibid., 138.

62 'was no longer the same': SS, 98.

62 'regained his own cheerfulness': Ibid.

63 'a period of darkness': ST, 114.

63 'without feeling the sweetness of it': Testimony of Céline Martin, ibid., 115.

63 'would previously have left her desolate': Ibid.

63 'complete conversion': SS, 98.

63 'filled with graces from heaven': Ibid.

63 'to please others': Ibid., 99.

64 'flowing from one of the divine hands': Ibid.

64 'from the eternal flames': Ibid.

64 'tall and handsome adventurer': SL, 66.

64 'first child': SS, 100.

65 'kissed the sacred wounds three times': Ibid.

65 'most dangerous age for young girls': Ibid., 101.

66 'doing me any harm': Ibid., 72.

66 'Céline did not rebel for one instant': Ibid., 106.

67 'heavenly expression': Ibid., 107.

67 'dear little father': Ibid.

67 'I defended myself so well': Ibid., 108.

67 'another soil more fertile': Ibid.

69 'commended her purity to St. Joseph': Testimony of Céline Martin, ST, 149.

69 'God's great mercy preserved': Testimony of Céline Martin, ibid., 151.

69 'one side of the carriage to the other': SL, 75.

70 'magnificence of the hotels and stores': SS, 130.

70 'carry off some souvenir': Ibid., 131.

70 'her limitless confidence': Ibid.

70 'ought to go aside to do': Testimony of Pauline Martin, ST, 57.

71 'both longed for and dreaded': SS, 132.

71 'everyone will agree!': Ibid., 135.

71   'if God wills it': Ibid.

71–72   'on the knees of Leo XIII': Ibid.

72   'at the bottom of [her] heart': Ibid., 136.

72   'to break down into sobs': *L'Univers*, November 24, 1887, LT, 376.

72   'a way of touching everything': SS, 139.

72   'in the blood of Jesus': Ibid.

72   'religious expression for women': Rudolph M. Bell, *Holy Anorexia* (Chicago: University of Chicago Press, 1985), 172.

72   'strange painful maladies': Ibid.

73   'who believes everything is permitted': SS, 138.

73   'do all he could': Ibid., 139.

74   'underhandedly': As described by Pauline Martin, letter to Isidore Guérin, December 10, 1887, LT, 384.

74   'to carry out his promise': Letter to Bishop Hugonin, dated December 16, 1887, ibid., 387.

75   'three months exile': SS, 143.

75–76   'repeats, 'Jesus, I love you!'': Pauline Martin, letter to Thérèse, dated November 23, 1887, LT, 358.

76   leaflet given the young pilgrim: LT, 336.

77   'tied with a sky-blue ribbon': SL, 84.

78   'nothing around me but sobs': SS, 147.

78   'it seemed impossible to walk': Ibid.

78   'disappoint [her] hopes': SL, 87.

78   'word burned like a torch': Sir. 48:2. *The New Oxford Annotated Bible with the Apocrypha* (New York: Oxford University Press, 1962), 192 (of the Apocrypha).

78–79   'nothing was too hard': Sir. 48:13. Ibid., 193.

79   'engaged in some other just occupations': Peter-Thomas Rohbach, O.C.D., *Journey to Carith: The Story of the Carmelite Order* (New York: Doubleday, 1966), 44.

79   'expression of the prophetic vocation': Ibid., 46.

80   'My daughter, what are you doing here?': Vita Sackville-West, *The Eagle and the Dove, a Study in Contrasts: St. Teresa of Ávila, St. Thérèse of Lisieux* (1943; reprint, London: Sphere Books, 1988), 134.

81 'rejected at a previous meal': Testimony of Pauline Martin, ST, 57.

81 'difficulty putting up with': Testimony of Marie de Chaumontel, ibid., 209.

81 daily cycle of devotions: See, for example, Acts 10:9, 16:25.

82 'exactly as I imagined it': SS, 149.

82 'in order not to turn back': Ibid., 237.

82 'mortify them and die to yourself': Testimony of Martha of Jesus, ST, 223.

83 'so happy in God's service?': Marie de Gonzague, in 1887 letter from Pauline Martin to Thérèse, LT, 286.

83 'loves her with all her heart': Postscript to a letter to Pauline, October 8, 1887, ibid., 290.

84 'without her even being aware of it': SS, 150.

84 'vexatious temperament of Mother Marie de Gonzague': ST, 95.

84 'whim of the moment': Ibid., 146.

84 'according to her fancy': Testimony of Thérèse's favorite novice, Marie Castel, ibid., 246.

84 'the wolf ': Ibid., 232.

84 'to avoid offending her susceptibilities': Ibid., 240.

85 'scatter a rain of sweets': Ida Friederieke Coudenhove Görres, *The Hidden Face: A Study of St. Thérèse of Lisieux* (New York: Pantheon, 1959), 167.

85 'magnificence of your gifts': Letter dated September 30, 1888, LT, 460.

85 'into acts of love': Testimony of Marie Castel, ST, 235.

86 'the least speck of dust': LC, 90.

88 'The monastery garden was white like me!': SS, 156.

88 'the sounds of cannon and the drum': Letter from Céline Martin to Pauline Romet, dated February 18, 1889, LT, 533.

89 'to suffer this way': Letter dated February 28, 1889, ibid., 537.

89 'needed one': Quoted in a letter from Céline Martin to her sisters in Carmel, dated March 9, 1889, ibid., 543.

89 'i.e., under my feet': SS, 160.

89–90 'ugly and the least convenient': Ibid., 159.

91 'by the breeze of love': Letter dated March 18, 1888, LT, 403.

91 prayer of General de Sonis: Translator's note, ibid., 407. Louis Gaston de Sonis (1825–1887), active in the Franco-Prussian War, was a Catholic military hero.

91–92 'as if someone lent me a body': LC, 88.

92 'Answer me, I beg you': Translator's note, LT, 571.

93 'but saying always: more more!': Letter dated March 13, 1889, ibid., 549.

93 'from us all that is most dear': Letter dated March 13, 1889, ibid., 552.

93 'they are never mystical': SS, 171.

93 'of which [she'd] never seen before': Ibid.

94 'take on irrevocable promises': LT, 645.

94 'father, tried by suffering': Ibid., 656.

95 'hold yourselves in readiness and to watch': SS, 168.

96 'absolute aridity': SS, 165.

96 'be willing to be nothing': Saint John of the Cross, quoted in William James, *The Varieties of Religious Experience* (1902; reprint, New York: Penguin Books, 1982), 506.

97 'simply laughed': SS, 166.

97 'flooded with a river of peace': Ibid.

97–98 'to give You joy and to console You': Ibid., 275.

98 'sadness and bitterness': Ibid., 167–68.

99 'she is a perfect religious': Letter dated September 9, 1890, LT, 678.

101 'read better than I did myself ': SS, 174.

101 'I actually flew': Ibid.

101–2 'heaven . . . unseen by anyone': Ibid., 170.

102 'three times with great emphasis': Ibid., 171.

102 'celebrated with a death': Ibid.

103 'did not have the least bit of fear': Ibid.

103 'to a better life': Ibid., 172.

103 'holding on only by a thread': Translator's note, LT, 733.

103 'draw out all the honey': Letter dated October 20, 1891, ibid., 741.

104 'as low as St. Mary Magdalene': SS, 83.

104 'a torrent of tears': Ibid., 176.

104 'Spouse placed on [her] forehead': Letter dated July 23, 1891, LT, 732.

104 'burn their wings': SS, 83.

104 'ardent love of creatures': Ibid.

105 'military type': Translator's note, LT, 733.

105 'beautiful': Translator's note, ibid.

105 'held each other closely and exclusively': Gibson, 93.

106 'to conduct her to her place': SS, 176.

106 'the most total incapacity': Letter to Thérèse dated August 17, 1892, LT, 756.

106 'cried all the time': Letter from Céline Guérin to her daughter Jeanne la Neele, dated May 10, 1892, ibid., 750.

106 'who then carried him': Translator's note, quoting Céline Martin, ibid., 751.

107 'what children do not understand and feel': Translator's note, quoting Céline Martin, ibid., 750.

108 'God wills to have you descend': Translator's note, quoting Céline Guérin, ibid., 757.

108 'no place to rest my head': Matt. 8:20.

108 'A question here of the interior': Letter dated October 19, 1892, LT, 762.

109 'new bud, gracious and scarlet red': PO, 38.

110 'into the arms of the Lord': SS, 238.

111 'it slips in everywhere!': Letter dated July 18, 1894, LT, 872.

111 'Everything about her commanded respect': ST, 218.

111 'temperaments she found hardest to bear': Ibid., 225.

112 'how much you have to lose': Sister Geneviève of the Holy Face, *My Sister Saint Thérèse* (Rockford, Ill.: Tan Books and Publishers, 1997), 28.

112 'the last stray of the family': Letter to her sisters in Carmel, dated July 3, 1893, LT, 792.

112 'I had become his mother': Ibid.

112 'always the dark night': Letter to Thérèse, dated July 12, 1893, ibid., 798.

114 'love can convert a soul': Letter dated May 22, 1894, ibid., 855.

115 'heart was no longer beating': Letter to her sisters in Carmel, dated June 5, 1894, ibid., 858.

115 'Then I am unhappy': Letter dated July 17, 1894, ibid., 868.

116 'into the immensity of heaven': Letter to her sisters in Carmel, dated July 29, 1894, ibid., 875.

116 'bosom of the divine Sun': Letter dated April 25, 1893, ibid., 786.

116 'Papa went *straight to heaven*': SS, 177.

117 'repugnance for the religious life': Translator's note, LT, 883.

119 'will be no longer any remedy': Letter dated October 21, 1894, ibid., 892.

119 'almost any form of unconventional behavior': René and Jean Dubos, *The White Plague: Tuberculosis, Man, and Society* (New Brunswick, N.J.: Rutgers University Press, 1952), 197.

120 'God can break iron just like clay': Letter dated July 18, 1894, LT, 871.

120 'accounts that we find so interesting': ST, 83.

120 'little poems to please everybody': Ibid.

121 'to much concentration on [her]self ': SS, 13.

121 did not include an Old Testament: Bible, IV, 26: 'French Versions,' in *New Catholic Encyclopedia* (New York: McGraw-Hill, 1967), 480–81.

121 'let him come to me': Prov. 9:4.

122 'forget myself and please others': SS, 99.

123 'Our mother said yes': Stéphane-Joseph Piat, O.F.M., *Céline: Sister Geneviève of the Holy Face* (San Francisco: Ignatius Press, 1964), 81.

123 'may my soul take its flight': SS, 276–77.

125 'so intense I thought I would die': ST, 63.

126 'when we love a thing the pain disappears': Letter dated September 17, 1896, LT, 999.

126 'the wicked are possessed by the devil': Undated letter to Thérèse, written about September 17, 1896, ibid., 997.

126 'must not stain the record': Translator's note, ST, 169.

127 'not even a stone': PO, 125.

128–29 'how right [her] little sister was': Translator's note, ibid., 121.

128 'you are the branches': John 15:5.

129 'in all its rigor': SS, 210.

129 'stream mounting to [her] lips': Ibid.

130 'conceal as much as it reveals': Michelle Perrot, ed., *A History of Private Life*, vol. 4, *From the Fires of Revolution to the Great War*, trans. Arthur Goldhammer (Cambridge: Harvard University Press, Belknap Press, 1990), 4.

130 'my soul was flooded with joy': SS, 210.

130 'with a great consolation': Ibid., 211.

131 'burn me away until nothing is left': These five lines are not from a single poem but are typical images taken from a number of Thérèse's verses.

131 'before reaching the age of thirty': Dubos, 59.

132 'slaves to fashion': Letter to Pauline, dated January 30, 1876, LT, 1221.

132 novels of the Far East: 'In *Dream of the Red Chamber*, said to be the first realistic novel in the Chinese language to be acknowledged as literature, it is the symptoms of tuberculosis that symbolize the emotional crisis of the heroine, Black Jade.' Thomas Dormandy, *The White Death: A History of Tuberculosis* (New York: New York University Press, 2000), 92.

133 need to be purified: For a discussion of tuberculosis as a metaphor for redemptive suffering in French literature, see David S. Barnes, *The Making of a Social Disease: Tuberculosis in Nineteenth-Century France* (Berkeley: University of California Press, 1995).

133 'therefore must be obliterated': Bell, 115.

133 'fervor'; 'first call'; 'transported': SS, 211.

135 'joyful days of the Easter season': Ibid.

135 'the thickest darkness;' 'living,' 'clear': Ibid.

135 'secrets of heaven': Ibid., 89.

135 'changed into a prayer': Ibid., 212.

136 'the night of nothingness': Ibid., 213.

137 'covers the starry firmament': Ibid., 214.

137 'already said too much': Ibid., 213.

137 'God is human loneliness': As cited by Bernard Bro, O.P., *The Little Way: The Spirituality of Thérèse of Lisieux* (London: Darton, Longman, and Todd, 1979), 5.

137-38 'declared that I looked well!': Letter dated July 16, 1896, LT, 969.

138 'left with love alone': Testimony of Teresa of Saint Augustine, O.C.D., ST, 195.

138 'what I want to believe': SS, 214.

139 calcify into nodules: The description of the typical course of tubercular infection is taken from Dubos.

139 'temptations against the faith': Testimony of Pauline Martin, ST, 43.

140 '*indifferent to Venerable Mother Anne*': SS, 192.

140 'produced from within': Ibid., 191.

140 'second SUNDAY of Mary's month': Ibid., 190.

140 'ever given to her child': Ibid., 191.

141 'at times a very small ray': Ibid., 214.

142 'forget what she owes you': Ibid., 215.

144 'the dew of humiliation': Ibid., 206.

144 'The little sister of a Missionary'; PO, 162.

144 'Or I am lost': Letter dated July 21, 1896, LT, 972.

144 'drawn down the grace of God': Letter dated April 29, 1897, ibid., 1089.

145 'This is perhaps your last retreat': Letter dated September 13, 1896, ibid., 991.

145 'sweep away transgressions like a cloud': Isa. 44:22.

145 'warrior, priest, doctor, apostle, martyr': SS, 192.

145-46 'I gain nothing': 1 Cor. 13:3.

146 'as for knowledge, it will pass away': 1 Cor. 13:8.

146 'a child of light': SS, 195.

146 'seeking by always stooping down': Ibid., 194.

146 'love is repaid by love alone': Ibid., 195.

147 'doing them by love': Ibid., 196.

147 'all other works together': Ibid., 197.

147 'Jesus alone sees': Undated letter, around September 8–17, 1896, LT, 991.

148 'I dread all that you love': Undated letter, around September 17, 1896, ibid., 997.

148 'ready to embark once more': Letter from Roulland, dated September 25, 1896, ibid., 1006.

149 'that served her as blankets': Ibid., 1027–28.

149 'inexorably causing her death': Translator's note, ibid., 1036.

149 'frightening': Letter to Céline Guérin, dated November 12, 1876, ibid., 1227.

150 'offered itself as victim': SS, 200.

150 'play without any suffering': LT, 1040.

150–51 'the glory / Of conquerors': 'To My Little Brothers in Heaven,' PO, 181.

151 'some relics of a future martyr': Letter dated February 24, 1897, LT, 1062.

151 'strangled and cooked in a pot': Ibid.

152 'interested and touched': Letter dated March 17, 1897, ibid., 1071.

152 'loved his family very much': LC, 46–47.

152 'Lend me your weapons': 'To Théophane Vénard,' PO, 192.

153 *nothing causes me alarm*: Ibid., 194.

153 'doing good on earth': LC, 102.

156 'still in our midst': Ibid., 22.

156 'an unbelievable effort to undress': PT, 73.

156 'defend or explain ourselves?': LC, 36.

157 'the means of remaining very little': Ibid., 37.

157 'kept up a sprightly conversation of banalities': Barry Ulanov, *The Making of a Modern Saint: A Biographical Study of Thérèse of Lisieux* (New York: Doubleday, 1966), 305.

157 'martyrs by desire and will': Letter dated May 9, 1897, LT, 1092.

157 'poor wandering Jew': Note to Pauline, around June 3, 1897, ibid., 1116.

158 'To be no more': PO, 203.

158 'to make God happy. Period': Translator's note, ibid., 202.

158 'any attachment here below': Letter dated May 23, 1897, LT, 1099.

158 'the letter is yours': Letter dated May 30, 1897, ibid., 1106.

158 'the little lamb was myself': Letter dated May 31, 1897, ibid., 1107.

158 'without being disturbed': SS, 227.

158 'swaying on their stems': Ibid., 228.

160 'impossible for me to go far': Ibid., 224.

160 'over such little things': Ibid.

161 'spinning around on the same pivot': Translator's note, LT, 1113.

161 'nothing on earth that makes me happy': Undated letter of June 1897, ibid., 1129.

161 'above all from creatures': Undated letter of June 1897, ibid., 1117.

161 'for self or for creatures': Letter dated June 9, 1897, ibid., 1127.

161 'the exile of the heart': SS, 218.

162 *humiliated, exiled ... withered:* Verbs culled from Thérèse's letters, autobiography, and poems.

163 'will have come to get me': June 5, 1897, LC, 57.

163 'to see my disappointment': May 15, 1897, ibid., 43.

163 'wants to give me': SS, 250.

164 'almost without sound': Thomas Mann, *The Magic Mountain* (New York: Vintage Books, 1969), 76.

164 'ghostlike envelope of flesh': Ibid., 348.

164 'pressed it to his lips': Ibid., 349.

164 'upper, spiritualized body': Susan Sontag, *Illness as Metaphor and AIDS and Its Metaphors* (New York: Anchor Books, 1989), 17.

165 'an indescribabaly pathetic beauty': Louisa May Alcott, *Little Women* (New York: Grosset and Dunlap, 1947), 484.

165 'glassful in a quarter of an hour': PT, 80.

166 "liked it to be up to there!": July 20, 1897, LC, 217.

166 'love over her physical exhaustion': LT, 1079.

167 'pour out His favors lavishly': Letter dated July 16, 1897, LT, 1145.

167 'joyful in the midst of suffering': Ibid., 1154.

167 'gnawing away at humanity': Ibid., 1162.

167 'in a similar hole': August 28, 1897, LC, 173.

167 'something joyful and sweet': July 30, 1897, ibid., 119.

168 'always had to be saying something funny': Ibid., 274.

168 'one always misses the train': Ibid., 277.

169 'I'll not miss all of them!': June 9, 1897, ibid., 62.

169 'heaven, and I'm announcing it': May 7, 1897, ibid., 42.

169 'cried all the way home': Letter dated May 14, 1876, LT, 1223.

169 'with the two little ones': Letter dated June 25, 1877, ibid., 1235.

170 'I did this with pleasure': July 8, 1897, LC, 79.

170 'never been at ease': July 30, 1897, ibid., 118.

170 'without failing in mortification': September 13, 1897, ibid., 189.

170 'Perhaps that's not good?': July 24, 1897, ibid., 108.

171 'not the candlestick, it's too ugly': Ibid., 284.

172 'I'll have nothing to write': September 7, 1897, ibid., 185.

173 'Don't talk of a date': July 31, 1897, ibid., 121.

173 'I'm dying from death!': August 3, 1897, ibid., 131.

173 'in the process of softening': PT, 86.

173 'reached its final stage': Ibid.

174 'except with terrible pains': Translator's note, LC, 162.

174 'I were on fire inside': Translator's note, ibid., 172.

174 All the better: August 16, 1897, ibid., 224.

175 'My pain was immediately doubled': ST, 160.

175 'almost universally used': Dubos, 63.

175 'That's the point!': August 18, 1897, LC, 152.

176 'obsessed with desire for them': ST, 57.

176 'kills the soul, life everlasting': Bell, 115.

176 'I'm dying of hunger': August 31, 1897, LC, 176.

177 'she began to cry': September 13, 1897, ibid., 189.

177 'the day of your death?': September 24, 1897, ibid., 199.

177 'receive your last look?': Undated, ibid., 229.

177 'hangs only on a light thread': September 26, 1897, ibid., 200.

177 'very heavy': September 29, 1897, ibid., 201.

178 'What must I do to die?': Ibid.

178 'confirmed in grace': SL, 203.

178 'I believe only in suffering': September 30, 1897, LC, 204.

178 'I can't take it, and that's it!': September 24, 1897, ibid., 198.

178 'it was her last agony': Ibid., 205.

179 'Am I not going to die? . . . My God I love you': Ibid., 206.

179 'to wound her again': Ibid., 207.

179–80   'twelve or thirteen years old': Ibid.

181   'to grant my desire': PT, 185.

181   'something in it for all tastes': Ibid.

182   'a very important work!': SS, xix.

182   'a cluster of red grapes': 'My Desires near Jesus Hidden in His Prison of Love,' PO, 134.

182   'wane of the romantic code': Perrot, 594.

184   'Don't lose one of them': September 14, 1897, LC, 190.

184   'timidly sent out the first spark': SL, 209.

184   'cut them up into tiny fragments': ST, 164.

184–85   '30,500,000 pictures and 17,500,000 relics': Görres, 393.

185   'You must heal me': Ulanov, 338.

SOURCES

Barnes, David S. *The Making of a Social Disease: Tuberculosis in Nineteenth-Century France.* Berkeley: University of California Press, 1995.

Bell, Rudolph M. *Holy Anorexia.* Chicago: University of Chicago Press, 1985.

Bro, Bernard, O.P. *The Little Way: The Spirituality of Thérèse of Lisieux.* London: Darton, Longman, and Todd, 1979.

Delaney, John J., ed., *A Woman Clothed with the Sun: Eight Great Apparitions of Our Lady.* New York: Image Books, 1961.

Dormandy, Thomas. *The White Death: A History of Tuberculosis.* New York: New York University Press, 2000.

Dubos, René and Jean. *The White Plague: Tuberculosis, Man, and Society.* New Brunswick, N.J.: Rutgers University Press, 1952.

Furlong, Monica. *Thérèse of Lisieux.* London: Virago Press, 1987.

Gaucher, Guy. *The Story of a Life: St. Thérèse of Lisieux.* New York: HarperCollins Publishers, 1987.

——. *The Passion of Thérèse of Lisieux.* New York: Crossroads Publishing, 1998.

Geneviève of the Holy Face, Sister [Céline Martin]. *My Sister Saint Thérèse.* Rockford, Ill.: Tan Books and Publishers, 1959.

Gibson, Ralph. *A Social History of French Catholicism, 1789–1914.* London: Routledge, 1989.

Görres, Ida Friederieke Coudenhove. *The Hidden Face: A Study of Saint Thérèse of Lisieux.* New York: Pantheon, 1959.

James, William. *The Varieties of Religious Experience.* 1902: Reprint, New York: Penguin Books, 1982.

O'Mahony, Christopher, ed. and trans. *St. Thérèse of Lisieux by Those Who Knew Her: Testimonies from the Process of Beatification.* Dublin: Veritas Publications, 1975.

Perrot, Michelle, ed. *A History of Private Life.* Vol. 4, *From the Fires of Revolution to the Great War.* Translated by Arthur Goldhammer. Cambridge: Harvard University Press, Belknap Press, 1990.

Piat, Stéphane-Joseph, O.F.M. *The Story of a Family: The Home of St. Thérèse of Lisieux.* Rockford, Ill.: Tan Books and Publishers, 1948.

———. *Céline, Sister Geneviève of the Holy Face: Sister and Witness to St. Thérèse of the Child Jesus.* San Francisco: Ignatius Press, 1997.

Sackville-West, Vita. *The Eagle and the Dove, a Study in Contrasts: St. Teresa of Ávila, St. Thérèse of Lisieux.* 1943. Reprint, London: Sphere Books, 1988.

Sontag, Susan. *Illness as Metaphor and AIDS and Its Metaphors.* New York: Anchor Books, 1989.

Thérèse de Lisieux, Saint. *St. Thérèse of Lisieux: Her Last Conversations.* Translated from the original manuscripts by John Clarke, O.C.D. Washington, D.C.: ICS Publications, 1977.

———. *Letters of Saint Thérèse of Lisieux.* Vols. I and II, *General Correspondence.* Translated from the original manuscripts by John Clarke, O.C.D. Washington, D.C.: ICS Publications, 1982, 1988.

———. *The Poetry of Saint Thérèse of Lisieux.* Translated by Donald Kinney, O.C.D. Washington, D.C.: ICS Publications, 1996.

———. *Story of a Soul: The Autobiography of St. Thérèse of Lisieux.* Translated from the original manuscripts by John Clarke, O.C.D. Washington, D.C.: ICS Publications, 1996.

Ulanov, Barry. *The Making of a Modern Saint: A Biographical Study of Thérèse of Lisieux.* New York: Doubleday, 1966.

Woodward, Kenneth L. *Making Saints: How the Catholic Church Determines Who Becomes a Saint, Who Doesn't, and Why.* New York: Simon and Schuster, 1990.

PERMISSIONS

Grateful acknowledgment is made for permission to reprint selections from the following copyrighted works: